Eruptions of Memory

Critical South
The publication of this series was made possible with the support of the Andrew W. Mellon Foundation.

Nelly Richard, *Eruptions of Memory*

Eruptions of Memory

The Critique of Memory in Chile, 1990–2015

Nelly Richard

Translated by Andrew Ascherl

polity

First published in Spanish as *Latencias y sobresaltos de la memoria inconclusa (Chile 1990–2015)* © Eduvim, Villa María, 2017, 1st ed.

This English edition © Polity Press, 2019

Polity Press
65 Bridge Street
Cambridge CB2 1UR, UK

Polity Press
101 Station Landing
Suite 300
Medford, MA 02155, USA

ISBN-13: 978-1-5095-3227-8
ISBN-13: 978-1-5095-3228-5 (pb)

A catalogue record for this book is available from the British Library.

Names: Richard, Nelly, author. | Richard, Nelly. Critica de la memoria, 1990-2010.
Title: Eruptions of memory : the critique of memory in Chile, 1990-2015 / Nelly Richard.
Description: Cambridge, UK ; Medford, MA, USA : Polity Press, [2018] | Compilation of essays, many of which originally published in: Critica de la memoria, 1990-2010. | Includes bibliographical references and index.
Identifiers: LCCN 2018019581 (print) | LCCN 2018034584 (ebook) | ISBN 9781509532308 (Epub) | ISBN 9781509532278 | ISBN 9781509532285 (pb)
Subjects: LCSH: Collective memory--Political aspects--Chile. | Protest movements--Chile. | Political violence--Chile. | Politics and culture--Chile. | Chile--History--1988-
Classification: LCC F3101.3 (ebook) | LCC F3101.3 .R534 2018 (print) | DDC 306.20983--dc23
LC record available at https://lccn.loc.gov/2018019581

Typeset in 10.5 on 12.5pt Sabon
by Fakenham Prepress Solutions, Fakenham, Norfolk NR21 8NL
Printed and bound in Great Britain by CPI Group (UK) Ltd, Croydon

For further information on Polity, visit our website: politybooks.com

Contents

Acknowledgments

Many people have contributed to this project, amongst them Andrew Ascherl, who has produced a careful and attentive translation; Sergio Villalobos-Ruminott (University of Michigan, Ann Arbor, USA) and an anonymous reader who reviewed the translation; and Graciela Montaldo (Columbia University, USA), who wrote the introduction, and Julia Sanches who translated it. At Polity, Sunandini Banerjee created a beautiful cover design and Neil de Cort oversaw the production process. The project was expertly managed by Paul Young at Polity and Ozge Kocak and Tristan Bradshaw at Northwestern University, USA. In addition, Penelope Deutscher (Northwestern University), thoughtfully shepherded the publication through its various stages.

The International Consortium of Critical Theory Programs gratefully acknowledges the Andrew W. Mellon Foundation for its support through grants to Northwestern University and the University of California, Berkeley, which have made possible the translation and publication of Nelly Richard's *Latencias y sobresaltas de la memoria inconclusa* (*Eruptions of Memory*) as part of the Consortium's *Critical South* series. Those involved in *Eruptions of Memory* thank the international editorial board of *Critical South*: Natalia Brizuela, Co-Chair (University of California, Berkeley, USA), Judith Butler, *ex officio* (University of California, Berkeley,

USA), Gisela Catanzaro (Universidad de Buenos Aires, Argentina), Victoria Collis-Buthelezi (WiSER, University of the Witwatersrand, South Africa), Souleymane Bachir Diagne (Columbia University, USA), Rosaura Martínez (Universidad Nacional Autónoma de México, Mexico), Leticia Sabsay, Co-Chair (London School of Economics and Political Science, United Kingdom / Universidad de Buenos Aires, Argentina), Vladimir Safatle (Universidade de São Paulo, Brazil), Felwine Sarr (Université Gaston Berger de Saint-Louis, Senegal), and Françoise Vergès (Collège d'études mondiales, France).

Finally, the project would not of course have been possible without Nelly Richard herself, who kindly made available the pre-published Spanish-language edition of the work and provided valuable assistance. Collaborating with several parties listed above, she nominated the translator and translation reviewer, liaised with her publisher, and provided the images that appear in this edition.

Anna Parkinson, Northwestern University

Translator's Note

A number of the citations in the original Spanish edition of this book refer to texts originally published in languages other than Spanish. I have endeavored in all of these instances to use published English translations (or the original English text as the case may be). All translations of Spanish language sources for which no published English translation is available are my own. Any explanatory end notes that I have added to this translation appear in square brackets [ ] and are signed "—Tr."

AA

Introduction:
The Struggle for Words

Graciela Montaldo, Columbia University

Translated by Julia Sanches

In Latin America, and especially in the Southern Cone, the 1970s were the setting for the greatest political and symbolic disputes of modern history. The emancipatory projects of revolutionary and grassroots movements and of the Leftist guerrillas that had been operating in the region since the 1960s (emboldened by the Cuban Revolution of 1959) were quashed by the brutal military and paramilitary repressions that began with the establishment of a civilian-military dictatorship in Uruguay on June 27, 1973. This was soon followed by a *coup d'état* in Chile, in which General Augusto Pinochet unseated Salvador Allende, the country's democratically elected president, on September 11, 1973. A handful of years later, on March 24, 1976, another military coup led to the foundation of a dictatorial government in Argentina. It was not long before the entire region fell under military rule (Brazil had been a dictatorship since 1964, and Bolivia and Paraguay each had decade-long dictatorships throughout the twentieth century). The dictatorial governments of these countries coordinated joint campaigns of repression under the umbrella of "Operation Condor," which counted on strategic support from the United States. These *coups d'état* were more than just new chapters in a long history of military interventions in the subcontinent's political life. Brutal repression, violence, disappearances, torture, and concentration camps that held thousands of detainees were all ways of breaking the people's will for radical change, and the cruelest form of domesticating citizens in order to pave the way for neoliberal and authoritarian policies that curbed people's rights and left many living in poverty.

Not only did the military coups of the 1970s interrupt democratic processes, they also imposed on society a new economic, political, and cultural model, implementing through it dynamics of repression and anti-politics. Class struggle – a historically active mode across Latin America – dwindled, social organizations were demobilized, and institutions (political parties, organizations, unions, grass-roots groups, and student movements) were dismantled. Workers, grassroots militants, and guerrilla fighters were rounded up in torture and detention camps alongside artists and intellectuals. All were affected by this brutal repression, which brought harm to the most destitute and to young middle-class militants in equal measure. For the politically progressive who were not disappeared, killed, or driven into exile, day-to-day survival under these conditions of terror begat a sort of double life: public life – silenced and devoid of political activity, except for some early human rights activism – and private life – in which they sought to preserve and reproduce critical thought and intellectual activity. Seeing in culture and art an enemy as dangerous as workers' rights movements and armed factions, military regimes attempted to tear down cultural networks by interfering in universities, censoring writers and their works, shutting down magazines and publishing houses, and imposing a widespread censorship that, of course, ended inevitably in self-censorship. Social practices were especially affected by the market's centrality and by the consumer policies dictated by neoliberal politics.

How was survival possible in those years? And, most of all, how did progressive society manage to reconstitute its ties and networks of solidarity and critique? In Chile, Argentina, and Uruguay, the small groups of intellectuals who remained played a decisive, dual role against their countries' respective military regimes: on the one hand, they would stand against the dictatorship – that is, they would reject the homogenizing discourse that aimed to suppress all divergent thinking; on the other, they would generate new systems of social exchange, bonds of solidarity, and social ties within dismantled societies whose cultural and political networks had been seriously impaired, and in which the market generated new mediations.

Southern Cone intellectuals and artists who created works during these dictatorships were the product of complex cultural experiences. In many cases, such as the case of Chile, these experiences intersected with the militancy of Leftist political parties and organizations, which carried out community services in traditionally excluded sections of society. Up until the 1970s, the Latin American Left had forged a symbolic alliance between artists, intellectuals, and the revolutionary subject par excellence, *the people* (an alliance that stemmed from populist movements). This alliance had found its definitive form in the Cuban Revolution and in the thinking of Che Guevara: "And to the professors, my colleagues, I will say the same: we must paint ourselves as blacks, mulatos, workers, farmers; we must go to the people, we must tremble with the people ..."[1] Dictatorships broke this sense of identification, and so the Left entered a process of profound self-reflection.

In the depths of their respective dictatorships, surviving artists and intellectuals began to contemplate new strategies of intervention and political positioning. The ideas of the people, of intellectuals, artists, and militants were subjected to critique, as was the system of political legitimation. In Chile, Nelly Richard played a relevant and unique role in defining the new position of art, artists, and intellectuals within dictatorial contexts, and in rethinking cultural practice in regimes of terror. The impact of her work was and remains enormous, not only in Chile, her adopted country (Richard was born in Caen, France, in 1948), but throughout Latin America. Her discourse not only appealed to art critics, philosophers, and social thinkers, but also to artists, writers, and curators. Her theoretical interventions changed the thrust of the discussions surrounding gender, art, memory, and politics in Latin America.

Against the dictatorship, the avant-garde

Nelly Richard settled in Chile in 1970, when the government of the Unidad Popular party (Popular Unity) came to power, with Salvador Allende as the country's president. Soon after her arrival, she held a position as the visual arts coordinator of the Museo Nacional de Bellas Artes. After Pinochet's *coup d'état* in 1973, Richard was removed from her position at the museum and, a few years later, in the late 1970s, became one of the most active intellectuals of what would later be referred to as the "Escena de Avanzada." The "Escena de Avanzada" consisted of a group of intellectuals and artists who, though different, were united by two premises: a radical opposition to the dictatorship, and an engagement with experimental aesthetic practices through avant-garde pursuits and the development of critical thinking. Richard had created a new, highly complex theoretical discourse which, rooted in a specifically Chilean context, aimed to provide an account of new political and cultural experiences. She opened up a space for debates on dictatorships, repression, censorship, victims' memories, the resignification of Leftist thought, the reorganization of feminist thought and gender issues, the aesthetic avant-garde within contexts such as that of Latin America, and the new space occupied by the market and consumerism in Chile. All of these experiences have in common the idea that intellectual and artistic practice have a political function that must, in turn, have a political effect in the public sphere. As such, the entirety of Nelly Richard's work can be read as an exploration of the relationship between aesthetics, culture, and politics, as is clear from the titles of most of her books. Neither nostalgic nor naive, her examination is carried out by way of a strong theoretical approach and through a search for categories and discourses which allow local experiences to be invested with new meanings. Her relationship with theory rejected the colonial model (which in Latin America had reproduced the thinking of hegemonic centers). In its place, Richard's theoretical practice gave rise to reflections on local phenomena while drawing on international critical thought. Richard also developed the concept of theory as a form of resistance against the widespread notion that reality could be easily represented in a manner that was "informative-communicative of immediate linguistic decoding" (*Crítica y política*, 163). This meant rejecting any interpretations put forth by the media that, coopted by the dictatorship, endorsed the image of model citizens as disciplined consumers. Regarding gender issues, Richard reoriented the traditional feminist debates in Latin America. Her work questioned the idea of gender as an identity to rethink feminism in the more general frame of oppression and dictatorial powers. In this context, the feminine would be a complex product of the mechanisms of appropriation, disappropriation, and contra-appropriation of the hegemonic practices. In Latin America, feminism used to be the result of activism and practical interventions in the public sphere. Richard introduced a strong theoretical approach. In doing so, she reappropriated a masculine tool (theory) and resignified the historical battles of women paying attention to the symbolic dimension.

After the experiences of the Latin American Left between the 1960s and early '70s, Richard's approach revisited and reworked the connection between culture and politics. It was no longer a matter of thinking politics as content and ideological discourse, but instead as a practice that ran permanently *against* the common sense of power, *against* institutions' (universities, museums, galleries, publishing houses, political parties) comfort zones, *against* the media's homogenization, *against* fixed subjectivities. Intellectuals and artists were the ones who, within this model, would have to generate interferences (in perception and thought), and question society, power, and community – not with political party slogans but through an act of permanent dislocation and critique. The discourse and aesthetics of the "Escena de Avanzada" rejected the notion of communicative transparency. The group's work was experimental; their critical discourse extremely theoretical and, at times, hermetic and opaque. Richard operated in the group as a sort of magnet, creating new meanings, introducing new topics, and directing the varying aesthetic practices toward the avant-garde. In this way, she resignified the role of curators and critics as sites for the production of discursivity, in collaboration with artists' creative work.

Members of the "Escena de Avanzada" worked across genres (visual arts, literature, poetry, video, cinema, critical texts) and expanded art's technical tools toward intermediality and the shifting dynamics of the processes of the city and the living body. The group grew out of the initiative of visual artists (Carlos Leppe, Eugenio Dittborn, Catalina Parra, Carlos Altamirano, the *Colectivo de Acciones de Arte* – or Art Actions Collective, otherwise known as CADA – Lotty Rosenfeld, Juan Castillo, Juan Dávila, Víctor Hugo Codocedo, Elías Adasme, among others) and their engagement with the written works of Raúl Zurita (poetry) and Diamela Eltit (prose); it also involved the participation of philosophers and sociologists such as Ronald Kay, Adriana Valdés, Gonzalo Muñoz, Patricio Marchant, Rodrigo Cánovas, and Pablo Oyarzún, among others.

The "Escena de Avanzada" was developed as an artistic avant-garde and was criticized for its emphasis on experimentation and theoretical discourse (drawing particularly on intellectuals such as Michel Foucault, Julia Kristeva, Gilles Deleuze, Félix Guattari, and Jacques Derrida). Chilean philosopher Willy Thayer voiced one of the more interesting polemics generated by the "Escena de Avanzada," arguing that the group's experimentation was complicit in Pinochet's dictatorial regime. The main point of his argument was that the group could not generate any real opposition to the dictatorship because the *coup d'état* had laid the foundation for its own rules of opposition, which allowed for the existence of an isolated avant-garde with little social intervention.[2] Richard took this objection seriously, responding: "This would mean that nothing exists *outside* the system and that, by extension, any act of criticism will always be implicated in the structures of power within which it seeks to generate disruptions of meaning" (*Crítica y política*, 37). In this sense, Richard's conception of the intellectual/artist is as a conspirator, as an entity operating within the system by employing some of its mechanisms, but instead using them against power, thus generating unrest, performing small acts of violence, shorting circuits, creating disconnections. The impact of Richard's first books may be described in similar terms. *Márgenes e Instituciones. Arte en Chile desde 1973. Escena de avanzada y sociedad* is a seminal study of the radical "Escena de Avanzada" artists and their function in dictatorial Chile (first published as a special issue of the Australian journal, *Art and Text*, in 1986).[3] In *La estratificación de los márgenes. Sobre arte, cultura y política/s* (1989), her second book, Richard analyzes new cultural practices, criticizing, precisely, their capacity for reification and institutionalization, and calling attention to the need to keep all emancipatory potential alive. Richard describes her interventions during that period with great clarity:

> The [Escena de] Avanzada responded to the annihilating nature of the military coup with a counter-coup, a barrage of images, materials, techniques and significations that explored forms of critical resistance in the face of totalitarian violence by *mixing with the present*, that is, by devising *process* and *relational* works (works that are not static, but *ongoing* and *situational*), whose openness, and in which the ephemerality of their signs allowed them to bypass – from the perspective of the living body, of biography or the city – the closure of what is finite and definitive in dead time, which is what grants museum paintings their eternity. (*Crítica y política*, 159)

The "Escena de Avanzada" remained very active throughout the 1980s.

The year 1990 was critical to Chilean history: after seventeen years of military rule, elections were held; a new phase began and, with it, a new government of "concili-ation" (consensus) led by Patricio Aylwin. This change would have profound consequences for Nelly Richard's work, as she saw the onset of democracy as a challenge to her continuing critical practice. That year, she would found and edit the influ-ential magazine *Revista de crítica cultural*, which appeared continuously until it ceased publication in 2008, with a total of thirty-six issues published. The magazine introduced the expression "cultural critique" as a form of repositioning oneself in relation to sociological approaches to culture and to the advance of cultural studies in American academia. By then, Richard was no longer just a critical/theoretical point of reference in Latin America; her colleagues in Latin American studies at US universities were starting to be drawn to the novelty and radicalness of her interventions. Although Richard spoke from the Left, she nonetheless questioned the essentialist tradition of politics and contemplated contem-porary society through the lens of new subjectivities, all in a sophisticated theoretical language. Unlike other intellectuals living in Latin America, Richard did not fashion her position in Chile – in the "margins" – into a place of power, but instead positioned it as a place for dialogue, debate, inquiry. Similarly, while the *Revista de crítica cultural* was still under her purview and backed by a group of intellectuals, Richard called on many younger people from different countries to join them in generating critical dialogues.

Throughout the 1990s, Richard published three influential books in Chile: *Masculino/Femenino. Prácticas de la diferencia y cultura democrática* in 1993, *La insubordinación de los signos (Cambio político, transformaciones culturales y poéticas de la crisis)* in 1994, and *Residuos y metáforas (Ensayos de crítica cultural sobre el Chile de la transición)*, written with the support of a Guggenheim grant, which she won in 1996, and published in Spanish in 1998. Like most of Richard's work, these books are made up of fragmented texts that simultaneously introduce new topics and debates while theoretically interrogating knowledge that was beginning to become institutionalized as the country underwent a transition to democracy. Along with the *Revista de crítica cultural*, whose highly avant-garde design – visually dynamic, it had a complex way of drawing readers in through the use of different fonts and the superimposition of images and texts that made reading it a kind of "work" – these three books went against what Richard refers to as "the linguistic tyranny of simplicity, directness, and transparency" (*Crítica y política*, 24). With the *Revista de crítica cultural*, Richard had wanted, in her own words, to "jolt the content of the theoretical pieces with graphic layouts that de-centralized their reading in favor of a reflexive visuality – far from all illustrative subordination – such that they could behave like just another text" (*Crítica y política*, 29).

In 2003, Richard and other intellectuals convened an international symposium to debate the status of culture thirty years after Chile's military coup. In her presentation of the event, she laid out the thrust of the debates: the relationship between art and politics. Richard sustained that the relationship between these had been historically shaped by two modes: socially engaged art and avant-garde art. Of course, her preference was for avant-garde art: "Unlike militant art, which purports to 'illustrate' its engagement with a political reality that is already invigorated by the forces of social transformation, avant-garde art aimed to anticipate and foreshadow change, using aesthetic transgression as an anti-institutional detonator" (*Arte y política*, 16). This statement also helps us to understand her critical work, which always sought to disrupt established meanings. Notwithstanding this penchant for disruption, Richard's writing continued to search for meaning in social practice, including aesthetic practice. Her contention with postmodernism, which had become widely popular in the social sciences and humanities of 1980s' Latin America, resides precisely in its commitment to cultural interpretation from the point of view of a deproblematized (postmodern) relationship with new trends in art and culture. For Richard, the search for meaning is always political; it requires the disruption of conventions and the existence of a kind of political, but also aesthetic, engagement with discourse that resists the temptation of linguistic transparency. Searching for meaning does not mean communicating clearly; on the contrary, it is a process within which arguments are made increasingly complex and ideas problematized. Richard's books are not straightforward but are committed to gener-ating dialogue and creating a relationship with readers and with other texts that give rise to conflicting views on the social. Herein resides the political dimension of this critical practice, which Richard prefers to refer to as "the political of" (rather than "the politics of") arts and culture.

The following works by Richard continue this line of thought. There is the edited volume of *Arte y política* (2005) the symposium on the thirty years that followed Pinochet's coup; *Fracturas de la memoria. Arte y pensamiento crítico* (2007); *Feminismo, género y diferencia(s)* (2008), in which she looks again at her critical reflections on gender theory in the context of new policies of social inclusion; *Crítica y política* (2013), an extensive interview that Richard rewrites in order to run through the fundamental themes of her work; and *Poéticas de la disidencia/Poetics of Dissent* (2015), a catalogue of the curatorial work she conducted on Chile's Pavilion at that year's Venice Biennale. One can trace a certain continuity in these works, not only in terms of their subject matter, content, and the issues raised therein, but also in that they contain an inter-pretative logic that runs counter to common sense (her dissident perspective is tireless), and a desire for intellectual engagement with critical thought that operates permanently against institutionalization and draws on other traditions of emancipation. Her books are all framed by a fragmentary perspective that, instead of moving toward a totalizing narrative, examines objects that might otherwise seem minor. The strength of her discourse lies in its disruption of official, overarching narratives, not with the aim of rendering them trivial through counter-narrative, but of revealing their fissures, in a way that is both deconstructive and grounded in political context.

On this note, it is worth mentioning that Richard has until now written her entire oeuvre in Spanish and, in so doing, has also, from this minority position – relative to the world of international theory – created a voice of dissidence with respect to the demands of the academic market. In creating spaces for dialogues and debates framed in different theoretical perspectives, she did so from a "situated" position, never losing sight of the fact that the objects in question are produced and circulate within a specific context and that critical voices inevitably take a stance; speaking from a position that is not aseptic nor indeterminate, these voices are instead heavy with the words of a specific community. Because of the significant impact Richard has had in the field of Latin American studies and American cultural studies, a number of her books have been translated into English (*Masculine/Feminine: Practices of Difference(s)*; *The Insubordination of Signs: Political Change, Cultural Transformation, and Poetics of the Crisis*; *Cultural Residues: Chile in Transition*). By the late 1990s, Richard began to work actively in the Universidad de Arte y Ciencias Sociales (ARCIS), in Chile, where she taught classes, founded graduate programs such as the degree in cultural criticism, and worked as the university's dean. Aside from her work at institutions, Richard continued, as always, to create new spaces in which to discuss current issues.

Eruptions of Memory

In 2010, Richard published *Crítica de la memoria (1990–2010)*. This book is a statement on a pivotal subject in Chile during that time period: a society's relationship with the memory of a dictatorship, with its traumatic and violent past, and with its present. *Eruptions of Memory: The Critique of Memory in Chile 1990–2015* returns to certain topics already present in *Crítica*, but with a number of rewritten chapters and new, revised materials on memory and its resignifications throughout the country's political history. To Richard, memory is *inconclusive*; it does not end, nor does it come to a close, because it is a political practice. The book begins by taking a definitive stance, in choosing how to refer to the period that began in 1990 when the first "democratic"[4] government came to power. Politicians referred to the process as a "democratic transition"; Richard prefers the term "post-dictatorship," therefore making it clear that the present remains anchored in that past, a past that continued to condition Chilean society. In this way, she brings into question the oversight that these new forms of power wanted to exert over the political process that had started with the elections. Her book also questions the idea of *consensus* as a model for national reconciliation – as expounded by Patricio Aylwin's government (1990) – and the Chilean Transition's official narrative of memory. During the 1990s, there was widespread debate throughout the Southern Cone on how to rethink dictatorial pasts – how to handle traumatic memories of violence, torture, the dismantling of a country's social fabric, and the loss of its revolutionary horizon. It was also during this decade that debates on both the traumatic memory of the Holocaust and the future of the Left after the fall of the Berlin Wall were rekindled across the globe.

Richard posits a controversial relationship with these debates and pens a highly personal book that positions itself beyond critical consensus. She holds that all stories about the past, including testimonies by human rights groups, must be revised in order to disrupt crystallized meanings. *Eruptions of Memory* stands against reconciliation in order to propose, in its place, a critical relationship with the past; a relationship in which the past could not be reified and in which the many meanings of the historical trauma that had changed Chile forever would remain open. While Aylwin's government conceived of a pacifying relationship with the past (and a large part of Chile approved of this tactic), Richard writes about what cannot be pacified (Chapter 1). However, she does so in fragments, selecting the objects of her pen from outside the overarching official narratives: the activation of memory during the detention of Pinochet in London (1998) and the media representation of the activism of pro- and anti-Pinochet women in Santiago streets (Chapter 2); the proliferation of testimonial texts of women who were tortured and of torturers (Chapters 3 and 4); the radical questioning of memory in the documentary films of Patricio Guzmán (Chapter 5); the architecture of memory and the resignification of official monuments throughout the inscription of the present in deterritorialized urban sites (Chapter 6); the publicity campaign for the 1988 plebiscite and the politics of images (Chapter 7); the updating of the dictatorial repression and the repression under democratic governments (Chapter 8); and the new theoretical challenges of the politics of memory forty years after Pinochet´s *coup d'état* (Chapters 9 and 10). Political readings do not have privileged objects of study but occur instead where there is discomfort, where social problems come into being. Richard sees aesthetic and intellectual practice as a matter of stance-taking and, therefore, as a struggle for the power to create meanings. Nevertheless, she distrusts the crystallization of meaning and supports a constant awareness of the present: "Criticism must demonstrate an awareness of the areas of greatest vulnerability and failures within the subsystem of which the dominant whole is composed so that interruptions can be generated, locally, altering the circuits of docile reproduction and integration" (*Crítica y política*, 37). Her entire unique and provocative oeuvre is contained within this maxim.

Bibliography

Avelar, Idelber. *The Untimely Present: Postdictatorial Latin American Fiction and the Task of Mourning*. Durham, NC: Duke University Press, 1999.

Beasley Murray, Jon. "Reflections in a Neoliberal Store Window: Nelly Richard and the Chilean Avant-Garde." *Art Journal* 64/3 (Fall, 2005), pp. 126–129.

Del Sarto, Ana. "Cultural Critique in Latin America or Latin American Cultural Studies?" *Journal of Latin American Cultural Studies* 9/3 (2000), p. 236.

Del Sarto, Ana. *Sospecha y goce: una genealogía de la crítica cultural en Chile*. Santiago de Chile: Editorial Cuarto Propio, 2010.

Guevera, Ernesto "Che." "Discurso al recibir el doctorado honoris causa de la Universidad Central de las Villas." https://www.marxists.org/espanol/guevara/59-honor.htm. January 2018.

Masiello, Francine. *The Art of Transition: Latin American Culture and Neoliberal Crisis*. Durham, NC: Duke University Press, 2001.

Oyarzún, Pablo, Nelly Richard, and Claudia Zaldívar (eds.) *Arte y política*. Santiago de Chile: Universidad Arcis-Universidad de Chile-Consejo Nacional de la cultura y las artes, 2005.

Richard, Nelly. *Márgenes e Instituciones. Arte en Chile desde 1973. Escena de avanzada y sociedad*. Documento Flacso n. 46. Santiago de Chile: Ediciones Metales Pesados, 2007. (1st ed. Melbourne: Art and Text/Francisco Zegers, 1986.)

Richard, Nelly. *La estratificación de los márgenes. Sobre arte, cultura y política/s*. Santiago de Chile: Francisco Zegers Editor, 1989.

Richard, Nelly. *Masculino/Femenino. Prácticas de la diferencia y cultura democrática*. Santiago de Chile: Francisco Zegers Editor, 1993. *Masculine/Feminine: Practices of Differences(s)*, trans. Silvia R. Tandeciarz and Alice A. Nelson. Durham, NC: Duke University Press, 2004.

Richard, Nelly. *La insubordinación de los signos (Cambio político, transformaciones culturales y poéticas de la crisis)*. Santiago de Chile: Editorial Cuarto Propio, 1994.

Richard, Nelly. *Residuos y metáforas (Ensayos de crítica cultural sobre el Chile de la transición)*. Santiago de Chile: Editorial Cuarto Propio, 1998.

Richard, Nelly. *Fracturas de la memoria. Arte y pensamiento crítico*. Buenos Aires: Siglo XXI, 2007.

Richard, Nelly. *Feminismo, género y diferencia(s)*. Santiago de Chile: Palinodia, 2008.

Richard, Nelly. *Crítica de la memoria (1990–2010)*. Santiago de Chile: Ediciones Universidad Diego Portales, 2010.

Richard, Nelly. *Crítica y política*. Santiago de Chile: Editorial Palinodia, 2013.

Richard, Nelly. *Poéticas de la disidencia/Poetics of Dissent: Paz Errázuriz – Lotty Rosenfeld*. Santiago de Chile: Polígrafa, 2015.

Richard, Nelly. *Latencias y sobresaltos de la memoria inconclusa (Chile 1990–2015)*. Córdoba: Eduvim, 2017.

Richard, Nelly and Alberto Moreiras (eds.) *Pensar en/la postdictadura*. Santiago de Chile: Editorial Cuarto Propio, 2001.

Thayer, Willy. "El Golpe como consumación de la vanguardia." *Extremoccidente* 2 (2003).

Prologue

The ten essays collected in this book encompass a sequence of processes and events connected to political and social memory in Chile: a sequence that begins with the democratic reopening marked by the 1988 plebiscite and covers the years of the Transition up to the mid-way point of Michelle Bachelet's second administration, taking into account the anti-neoliberal rupture of the student movement that in 2011 provoked a broad, popular questioning of the market society model promoted by successive Concertación governments.[1] This book reviews the political and social moments of dictatorship, Transition, and post-Transition, unraveling and recommencing the modalities of remembrance that inhabit the different politics and poetics of memory.

This sequence of democratic governance (1990–2015) serves as the backdrop for the ebb and flow of a memory that is replete with setbacks: a memory whose slogan, "truth, justice, and reparations," both achieved success and suffered severe defeat. It is well known that the balance sheet of memory can never be considered to have been won and that the stages of the traumatic recollection of the military dictatorship are full of intermittencies, convulsions, erasures, resurgences, and new omissions, leakages, and cracks. The conditions of the production of historical recollection vary according to the fluctuations of a memory that must not regard the past as if it were already concluded but rather as a network of half-open significations that, in its gaps and interstices, is interpellated by the contingency of a vigilant and expectant present. The unstable relationship between past(s) and present acquires expressive vigor and communicative power by situating the recollections of yesterday in a vital resonance with contemporary anxieties and concerns.

The official script of memory organized by the Chilean Transition (a script based on the rhetoric of consensus that, in the name of an always threatened governability, sustained the "democracy of agreements") was characterized by "reconciliation," with its moral symbology of forgiveness. The texts in this book record what occurred in relation to human rights in Chile (Pinochet's international arrest; protests by the Agrupación de Familiares de Detenidos Desaparecidos [Association of Relatives of Disappeared Detainees] (AFDD) against unfulfilled promises of justice; the demarcation of "places of memory" and the creation of the Museo de la Memoria y los Derechos Humanos [Museum of Memory and Human Rights]; the commemoration of the fortieth anniversary of the military coup and the subsequent media explosion of the archives of memory, etc.), while maintaining a concentrated focus on those residual particles of a convulsive, unreconciled memory that tumultuously exceed the frame of institutional memory.

At the fraying edges of the discursive production of order – neoliberal Chile's technocratic rationality and its knowledge of planning and management – one still finds floating traces of this historical disaster (the 1973 coup and military dictatorship), which the official balance sheet of a well-administered Chile refuses to recognize. The narratives of demilitarization, which still provoke resentment because of this break in history, do not conform to the explanatory matrix of the professional sciences (economics, sociology, political science, communication) that has become the official language of the Transition. This pragmatic language of democratic realism excludes from its technical diagnostics the resistant shadows of the imaginaries wounded by the dictatorship's violence. Perhaps only the symbolic constellations of aesthetic creation and critical thought are able to make the labor of memory pass through the gaps in

historical temporality and in the failures of social representations. Unlike the executive knowledge of the professional
sciences, cultural criticism feels closer to the experiences of
loss and precariousness that underscore the abrasive textures
of social conflict. Out of the residues and opacities of the
symbolic, cultural criticism speaks a language that is broken
enough that the cracks within its vocabulary and categories
constitute a bond of solidarity with the most grievously
injured domains of the painful past. Cultural criticism's
freedom to cross boundaries allows it to infiltrate zones
of contact and friction that other social practices, cultural
symbolizations, media constructions, forms of citizen intervention, and aesthetic models cannot, as they are unable to
integrate themselves easily into the same landscape due to the
academic protocols that delimit subjects and objects of study
according to the division of specialized disciplines. Moreover,
the essayistic practice that pertains to cultural criticism (with
which this book identifies) resists and opposes the functional
and utilitarian grammars so expertly used by institutional
politics and the marketplace of knowledge to pay tribute to
a techno-administrative order that, armed with the language
of neoliberal consensus, allows no form of expression for
those subjectivities who are troubled by and disagree with the
neoliberal consensus.

The texts in this book are critical of the way in which the
Transition's official apparatus, by seeking to neutralize the
polemical energy of memory with its script of moderation
and resignation, obliterated conflicts of interpretation that
must remain alive in memory so that, thanks to the insubordination of signs, the past can be kept in a permanent state
of actuality. Yet these texts are also interested in practicing
a critique of memory that teaches us that not all forms of
reconfiguring the past to make public memory consistent
are equivalent, however much they may be motivated by a
common desire to struggle against forgetting, to condemn
the violations of human rights that occurred during the
dictatorship, and to honor the victims of torture and disappearance. Every production of memory – as it is determined
in documents, archives, testimonies, confessions, architectures, etc. – should be judged according to the kind of
symbolic and narrative operation that modulates the relation

between event, experience, narration, voice, and social discursivity. The work of cultural criticism helps to contrast the different enunciative constructions that rhetorically and politically support every model of memory by examining the intentionality of the perspectives that select fragments of remembrance, orient the gaze toward particular images, and frame the scenes of the story that contains them. Thus, the critique of memory must revise the different assemblages of meaning that support images and stories in order to discriminate between, on the one hand, conciliatory evocations of a seamless past that seek the consolation of a sutured memory and, on the other hand, work divided by the insubordinate memory that distrusts all commemoration of the past (even if it is the heroic past of the victims) because of how it excludes the discordant fragments of an inherently plural recollection. In its examinations of the operations of meaning, cultural criticism makes it possible to distinguish between the representational and counter-representational apparatuses that can be identified with either contemplative memory (a memory recorded in the static image of a literal past) or transformative, non-mimetic memory (a memory that heterogeneously combines its archives and testimonies according to the different times, places, and modes in which the memory being convoked by the present is resignified). This memory, with its intersections and bifurcations, finds itself today at a new crossroads (neoliberalism/anti-neoliberalism), one in which the very historicity of the social is at stake. It invites us to take a position with regard to the complex ways in which the past traverses into the present in order to contribute to the critical awakening of an emancipated subjectivity.

1

Traces of Violence, Rhetoric of Consensus, and Subjective Dislocations

The first governmental administration of Chile's Transition to democracy (led by Patricio Aylwin in 1990) constructed itself on a consensus-based model of a "democracy of agreements." This model signaled a shift from politics as antagonism (the drama of the conflict was exacerbated by the polarizing confrontation between the dictatorship and its opponents) to politics as transition (the formation of agreements and the technicalities of negotiations conducted by new institutional authorities and the entrenched powers that remained hidden in the shadows, continuing to block the path toward democratic recovery).[1] The "democracy of agreements" made consensus its normative guarantee, its operational code, its de-ideologizing ideology, its institutional rite, and its discursive victory.

What kind of excesses did this new rhetoric of consensus seek to control by attempting to force unanimity, through formally and technologically rationalized democratic agreements, onto the voices of those who fought against the dictatorship? Excessive *vocabularies* (the dangerous riot of words disseminating heterodox meanings in order to name the hidden/repressed that trespasses into the networks of official discourse); excessive *bodies* and *experiences* (the discordant modes in which social subjectivities break the identifying lines drawn by political scripts or advertising spots); excessive *remembrances* (the tumultuous reinterpretations of a past full of aspirations and defeats – of Unidad Popular [Popular Unity] and the military coup of 1973 – that keep the memory of this history open to an incessant struggle of readings and meanings).

Memory and disaffection

The recuperation and normalization of the democratic order in Chile was an attempt to exorcise the ghosts of the multiple ruptures and dislocations of life produced by the coup and the military dictatorship, employing the consensus method to neutralize the differentiating counterpoints, antagonistic postures, and polemical demarcations of conflicting meanings through a politico-institutional pluralism that assumes a noncontradictory diversity. This nonconflictive diversity is a passive sum of differences that are almost indifferently juxtaposed, and it avoids any confrontation between these differences so as to forestall any disruption of a neutral reconciliation of opposites. The terms *pluralism* and *consensus* were summoned by the architects of the democratic transition to represent a new society in which the official channels of expression only bothered to honor diversity when it was in line with the Transition's carefully calculated agreements, thus avoiding any attempt to reckon with the ideological conflicts of the past.

Consensus, the paradigm of political legitimacy, was established in order to normalize the heterogeneous plurality of the social. This was a model that disciplined antagonisms and confrontations and established rules designed to protect macro-institutional agreements. The Transition's official consensus excluded from its national protocol the memory of conflicts that took as their basis and passion the internal struggle around the meaning of the "transition to democracy," apparently forgetting that all supposedly neutral social objectivity is a threatened objectivity. It "necessarily presupposes the repression of that which is excluded by its establishment."[2] The Transition's official discourse disregarded the negative force of the excluded and prevented the polemical and controversial vitality of the repressed from disturbing the limits of normalized politics. To avoid impeding the regulation of the pre-established connections between memory, violence, and democracy, the Transition suppressed from its repertoire of *accepted* meanings the *inconvenient* memory of what preceded and exceeded the politico-institutional consensus.

Claiming that "consensus is the highest stage of forgetting," Tomás Moulian alludes to the "whitewashing" that, during the Transition, began to sweep away sharp contradictions about the historical value of the past and to smooth over disagreements about the objectives of a transitional present in which "politics no longer exists as a struggle of alternatives, as historicity." During the Transition, politics functioned instead as a "history of small variations, adjustments, changes in aspects that do not compromise the global dynamic."[3] These "small variations, adjustments, and changes" heralded a society with a predetermined future. This democratic realism was an attempt to move away from the risks of indeterminacy at the cost of further lowering the expectations of a social body that no longer felt attracted to the once radiant field of decisions and historical wagers.

The official administrators of consensus success-fully downplayed the marks of violence that have always been attached to the name "post-dictatorship" in order to downplay the seriousness of the meaning conveyed in their staging of the "facts," neutralizing it with the professional vocabulary of "transition." The rhetoric of consensus decreed that nothing intolerable, nothing insufferable, should ruin the spirit of wanting to facilitate the reconciliation of society. During the Transition, the political meanings of memory were once again rendered inoffensive through the use of words stripped of both emotion and fear. Even if the Transition's discourse occasionally alluded to memory as conflict, it was not able *to express its agony*. Moreover, immediate suspicion was generated by the symbolic density of any testimonial narrative whose figurative language could, in spite of this catastrophe, still generate an emotional outpouring of memory that altered the meticulously studied formulism of the exchange between politics and the media.

The Transition-era administrations followed a consensus-oriented script that turned memory into a solemn yet

almost painless citation. Their evocation of memory failed
to mention all the material injury of the past: its psychic
density, its experiential volume, its affective trace, and its
scarred backgrounds, the pain of which is diminished neither
by the merely compulsory method of the judicial process nor
by official memorial plaques. Public discourse during the
Transition attempted to pay off its debts to the past formally
without expressing too much regret, almost without reflecting
at all on the repulsiveness, torture, hostility, and resentment
that continue to rip apart living subjects. Like many words
that are intended to circulate innocently – without weight or
gravity – throughout the communicative pathways of media-
saturated politics, the word "memory" seems to have erased
from its public expression the intolerable, antisocial memory
of the nightmare that tortured and persecuted subjects during
the dictatorship.[4] The word "memory," thus recited by the
mechanized speech of consensus, subjected the memory
of the victims to yet another outrage, once again making
them insignificant by allowing their names to be spoken
in a language weakened through official routines that had
previously guarded these identities from any investigations
into the convulsions and fractures of history. Reduced to the
meaningless language of objective certification, a few words
testify only to the number of victims. The intolerable aspects
of memory are not allowed to disrupt the expressive rules
of the language used to refer to it. The consensus-oriented
method of the "democracy of agreements" prohibited any
eruption of voices that could reveal the paroxysms of rage
and desperation felt by the victims' families.

Biographical ruptures, narrative disarticulations

The experience of the post-dictatorship binds the social
body's individual and collective memories to figures of
absence, loss, suppression, and disappearance. These figures
are surrounded by the shadows of a suspended, unfinished,
and tense mourning that leaves the subject and the object
in a state of sorrow and uncertainty, ceaselessly wandering
around that which is inaccessible in the body, as well as

around the truth that both the subject and the object lack (it is absent) and need (they miss it).

In the most brutally sacrificial dimension of violence, the bodies of the missing are evoked by absence, loss, suppression, and disappearance. They also connote the symbolic death of a social historicity whose mobilizing force is no longer recoverable in its utopian form. This force of historicity survived during the dictatorship as a struggle over meanings, as a struggle to defend an imperative and urgent meaning in combat against the military regime. The conditions of existence had to be reinvented in order to survive the catastrophe of the dictatorship. Undoubtedly, the epic task of confronting everything as a matter of life and death, every act as dangerous, entailed increasing the rigor applied to practices and identities. Such overexertion ultimately resulted in exhaustion. Today, many are tired of the heroic discipline and combatant-centered maximalism that once demanded their fidelity, now preferring instead to content themselves with small, neo-individualist, personal, everyday satisfactions. Such partial tactics of isolation and distraction create the illusion of certain "relative autonomies in relation to the structures of the system" when it is no longer reasonable to believe in the imminent demise of this system.[5]

However, the democratic transition and its normalizing networks of order also deactivated the exceptional character of the quest for meaning as it was presented to us at the moment of struggle against horror and terror in zones of life and thought in a state of emergency. Extremism had been expressed previously through the defense of irreplaceable (absolute) truths. During the Transition, it became part of the regime of the flat substitutability of signs with which (in the name of evaluative relativism) neoliberal society de-emphasized the desire and passion for change.[6] Whatever the painful motive for this renunciation may be, the post-dictatorial condition is expressed as the "loss of an object" in a situation marked by "mourning":[7] psychical blockages, libidinal withdrawals, affective paralyses, inhibitions of will and desire in the face of the sense of having lost something unrecoverable (body, truth, ideology, representation). Post-dictatorship thought, as Alberto Moreiras argues, is "more suffering than celebratory" because, "like the mourning that must fundamentally both assimilate and expel, thought attempts to assimilate the past, seeking to reconstitute itself, reform itself, following lines of identity with its own past; but it also tries to expel its dead body, to eliminate its tortured corruption."[8] This melancholic dilemma between "assimilation" (remembering) and "expulsion" (forgetting) marked the post-dictatorial horizon with narratives split between silence (the lack of speech connected to the stupor resulting from a series of unassimilable changes to the subject's continuity of experience due to the velocity and magnitude of these changes) and overexcitation (compulsive gestures that use artificially exaggerated rhythms and signals to combat the tendency toward depression). At one extreme we find biographies imprisoned by the sadness of an unmovable memory in its morbid fixity, and, at the other extreme, light stories that emerge hysterically through the over-agitation of the quick and the fleeting in order to achieve trivial media recognition. From silence to over-excitation; from bewildered suffering to the spoken simulation of a supposedly recovered normality: these responses to tragic memory reveal, consciously or unconsciously, the problematic status of historical memory in the post-dictatorship era. It is a memory that must avoid both the nostalgic petrification of yesterday in the repetition of the same and the marketed choreography of diversity that exhausts itself in futile variations on the novelty of change.

The destitution of history as volume and event and its anodyne replacement by the flat surface of consensus and its anemic mechanisms of meaning have generated, in some social actors, an intensified nostalgia for the anti-dictatorship movement, retroactively giving it an epic, self-referential meaning. The mythologization of the historical past as a symbol of the purity and untaintedness of political ideals led to the victims' sanctification. This attempt to redress the paucity of heroic examples in a present devoid of any protest thereby surrenders to the pragmatism of actions with no interest in moral rebellion. During the dictatorship, the weakening of that universe of clearly defined meaning through stark oppositions between officialdom and dissidence locked in a tragic battle disastrously resulted in an abhorrence of all utopianism. Hence the post-dictatorship subject's melancholic-depressive symptom, which leaves her sadly submerged in decay, in the silence and inaction of retreat, without the vital stimuli for articulating responses to senseless threats.

Lost was the historical macro-referentiality of polarized, oppositional struggle and the relativist fragmentation of the values characteristic of the post-dictatorship horizon. Some experienced this as a liberating downfall of totalizing truths that broke with an oppressive ideological creed and its doctrinaire hierarchy. However, in the biographies of militants these ruptures were rendered in a particularly vivid way as a panicked disorientation in the face of the explosion of the interpretative coordinates that had once ordered their visions of the world according to the univocal contours of homogeneous centralities and totalities. They were left without any certainty of identity or belonging. The landscape of the Transition was filled with diffuse borders and continuous margins, with oblique mechanisms and scales of oscillating values that no longer required choosing sides from among ethically opposed options. A map of opportunistic conversions caused biographies and identities to change. The permutation of services and commodities under neoliberalism shares a similarly rapid rhythm, requiring no consistency from anyone.

The utopian horizon of the previous anti-establishment struggle – a horizon that was to see itself betrayed by the adaptive conformism of the new social roles aligned with political power and economic success – reflected traumatic fractures that inhibited the recollections of memory by censoring the connections between the past and present in order to thereby hide the moral gaps that divide the lives of the former militants who were "converted" by history.[9]

The official Chilean transition to democracy made use of society's discomfort with memory and the self-censorship with which its protagonists severed the ties between "before" and "after." This protected the immediate present from any charge of infidelity or incoherence. Taking advantage of a tersely circumscribed here and now without historical connections, the Transition saturated this present with the fleeting and transitory disengagement of immediate rhythms and virtues so that history would be definitively forgotten. Likewise, instantaneity and momentariness are the frivolous means with which the Transition's novelty disguised the temporary ambivalence of its game of masks between the present of democratic reopening and the past of military authoritarianism. The first Transition administration may have signaled its estrangement from and rupture with the antagonistic world of the dictatorship, but its neoliberal democracy was entirely complicit with the hegemony of the market. This guaranteed the continuation of the military regime's modernizing policies, considered successful by several converts. Put differently: in the present, the Transition had to emphasize the political and democratic "novelty" of its "discourse of change" in order to silence the non-new (the inherited) of the economic and military forms extending from the dictatorial past. Obscured by the Transition, this perversion of temporalities indistinguishably mixed continuity and rupture. This took the form of incessant self-affirmation as *actuality*: the exhibitionist pose of a truncated past–present.

The presence of the memory of absence

Tracing, unearthing, exhuming the remnants of the past: these are the actions that human rights groups have ceaselessly carried out, defying the sinister intelligence of a power that erased the evidence (the remains) of its criminality in order to prevent any kind of material verification of its actions. Tracing, unearthing, exhuming: these all mark the desire to make the missing pieces of bodies and truths reappear, to bring together archival evidence, documents, and testimonies that will once and for all finish what justice has left incomplete.

The remains of the disappeared and the remains of the past that has disappeared must first be discovered (dis-covered) and then assimilated. This is to say, they must be reinserted into a biographical and historical narrative that admits loss and weaves around it restorative coexistences of meanings. In order to unblock the memory of the past that pain or guilt has encrypted in a sealed temporality, we must liberate diverse interpretations of history. The unstable temporality of their multiple, disconnected fragments can demonstrate new versions and rewritings of what took place. The event is thereby relocated in unexpected networks of historical intelligibility. Thus, it is not a matter of turning our attention back toward the dictatorship in order to record a contemplative image of what was suffered and resisted. It is not a mythical recollection, but rather a reopening of fissures in the blockages of meaning which history can consider neither finite nor definitive.

The memory of the wounded past is most dramatically conjugated in the double hybrid narrative of the disappeared and their families who struggle against the absence of their bodies and thus must incessantly produce the social *appearance* of the memory of *disappearance* in a fragile story that is always under the threat of invalidation. Faced with the body's absence, the recollection of identity is prolonged by the story's symbolic construction. This keeps the memory of the missing person alive, ensuring that they do not "disappear" again by being forgotten. "The suffering of memory is used to give life to death."[10] It is thus a matter "of life or death" that the families' recollections of the victims endure. Their determined obsessiveness cannot be dissuaded from repeating the charges against the perpetrators, so as to concede nothing to oblivion. Hence the indefatigable recollection of the traumatic event, which reiterates loss, re-marks it, thus contradicting (through saturation) the absence of any trace of the social and political mechanism of disappearance that facilitated the material suppression of bodies. Hence, as well, the multiplication of symbolic acts of remembrance by the victims' families that redefine memory against the indeterminacy of uncertain death. The *will to make memory present* opposes the *present unwillingness to remember* through a litany that is "infinitely reiterated like a monotone chant," its repetition attempting to "exorcise the name being evoked from oblivion."[11]

But in what language can we hear memory's desperation and its irrepressible demand for presence, given the banalization of memory and the present by the dehistoricizing techniques of a heavily mediated world that has broken all individual and collective bonds between *politics* and *meaning*?

Consensus belongs to the various techniques of forgetting that call for the past to be disregarded. Its postulates of order and social reintegration exclude the bothersome dissimilitude of "them" from the carefully policed limits of similitude and homogeneity of reconciliation's "us." The excluded "them" embody the past, they bear its stigmas on their living flesh, refusing to cover these scars with media and entertainment spectacles and the cosmetics of well-being. There are also institutional policies for the obliteration of guilt. Truth is separated from justice in a declared disconnection from ethical claims about perpetrators. Those who have been identified should not benefit a second time from the same perverse operation: the concealment of identities and the evasion of responsibilities. In addition, secret associations are woven between business agreements and networks of convenience by the dissipated forms of forgetting produced daily by mass media. Neither memory nor its suppression will be noticed in the midst of so many fine, invisible forms of censorship restricting and distorting the fields of vision and knowledge.

The victims' families know the difficulty of keeping the memory of the past alive and *conscientious* when all the rituals of consumerism conspire to distract it. Hence the interminable list of declarations, acts, and notices that the Agrupación de Familiares de Detenidos Desaparecidos [Association of Relatives of Disappeared Detainees] (AFDD) regularly publishes in its annual "Summary of Activities." Hence the documentation of the neurotic tasks that multiply along the path toward truth and justice, which victims' families attempt to reconstruct in their anxious, daily production signals and objective messages that substitute for and fill the subjective void of the disappeared's absence. The desire to memorialize and commemorate the loss that the victims' families want to keep alive collides with the passive universe of sedimented indifference, a universe combining machinations and spontaneities, calculations and automatisms, impositions and dispositions. Together, they produce the meaningful expenditure of communitarian acts and words that had, prior to the Transition, been charged with rigor and emotion. The memory of "Where are they?" can no longer find a place in a landscape devoid of intensive narratives or vocal dramatizations. Germán Bravo has reflected on this drama's immateriality in relation both to the AFDD testimonies and to the difficulty of inscribing this problematic of memory in Transition-era Chile. It seems these cries can only be heard as "a boring chant, a chant that has now lost all sound, all change in tone, a name ... confronting the stature of time with only the force of its repetition. The infinite repetition of an intolerable name. Of a name that has become inexpressible and inaudible."¹²

The AFDD argues that "justice is non-negotiable." This is to say, "the pain of each and every one of us cannot be quantified." The *experience* of pain would thus be unquantifiable, irreducible to the market's law of exchangeability, a law designed to flatten qualities and properties so that they can be more easily converted to the neutral regime of equivalence of the commodity form and the sign. However, how can the value of experience (the lived material of the singular and the contingent, the testifiable) be demonstrated if the lines of force of consensus and the market have standardized subjectivity and technologized speech to the extent that it is increasingly difficult for the irreducible singularity of historical events to interrupt the passive uniformity of the passing of time? Where can the most terrifying aspects of memory be recorded if hardly any surfaces remain for the inscription of memory, for the relocation of meaning, and for saving it from the crudeness, maliciousness, and indifference of ordinary communication?

2
Women in the Streets:
A War of Images

The Transition government that came to power in Chile in 1990 based its political horizon of consensus on grammars of moderation and resignation that promoted an image of uniform temporality, an undefined place where no plans are interrupted and no shocking events occur. Democratic formalism and its protocols of governability guaranteed that the administrative machinery of institutional politics would control the social, homogenizing its flows of expression and opinion under the vaguely civic designation of "the people." There would be no imbalance of tone or behavior to alter the mechanized programming of a present without risk or uncertainty, and thus the Transition government and the uniformed guards of institutional order formulated their agreement to a "controlled democracy." Nothing remained that could predict the failure of this rational pragmatism, coordinated by military, economic, political, and media apparatuses that guaranteed the instrumental precision of the diverse mechanisms that composed the refined systems and subsystems of the Transition, when suddenly something took on the force of an *event*: the surprise arrest and detention of ex-dictator and then Senator-for-Life Augusto Pinochet in London on October 16, 1998.[1] This invasive and disruptive event upset the predictable routine, dislocating the efficient series of arrangements and calculations of the transitional

regime's political formulism. Although the conventional
political machine quickly attempted to reabsorb the disorder
of signification that the "Pinochet event" generated back into
its language of governmental interests, multiple incongruous
flows of expressivity nevertheless managed to disseminate
themselves throughout the social. When the landscape of
the Transition appeared to be definitively saturated by the
predictability and routine conformism of the limits imposed
by democratic reasonability, the "Pinochet event" detonated
its explosive charge outside the hegemonic definitions of the
administrative practice of politics.

Reports of Pinochet's arrest and detention threw the
national news media's playbook into disarray, drawing
attention instead to images and memories that had long been
prohibited by the tacit media censorship of memories of the
dictatorship during the first years of the Transition. Some
of these images and memories had been prohibited by the
transitional regime's efforts to de-intensify the past in order
to neutralize the inherent conflicts of the act of remembering.
With the "Pinochet event," history and memory abruptly
became zones of media-oriented performativity, political
enunciation, and social intervention. Both amateur and
professional-quality footage of the street protests reacting
to the news of Pinochet's arrest provided television cameras
with images of bodies finally free to demonstrate their violent
opposition to the extremism, indignity, and indignation that
once again brought supporters and opponents of the military
government into confrontation with one another.

Several events broadcast by the media are worth mentioning,
particularly the series of opposing protests by women in the
streets of Santiago: on one side, women who had been called
on by Pinochet loyalist groups to violently and stridently
demand the liberation of the ex-dictator from his detention
in London; and, on the other side, the victims' families, who
demanded that Pinochet be prosecuted as the main perpetrator of state terrorism, torture, and disappearances.

The groups of Pinochetista women protesting in the streets
of Santiago inevitably called to mind the marches organized
by Poder Femenino [Women's Power], a group that fought
against Salvador Allende during the Unidad Popular era.
It is no coincidence that femininity is the thread running

through the zone of conflict between history and memory that connects the Pinochetista women of today with the right-wing counterrevolutionary women of yesterday. It is not because women function as a privileged signifier of the tension between order and revolt when crisis threatens a society's progress and the legitimacy of its systems, or when the contradictions between modern values and regressive values are intensified. Rather, the feminine presence in crisis situations in Chilean history signals time and again the contradiction between *containment* and *excess* focused on by women to reaffirm or even transgress the balance of political reason when called forth, especially by a traditionalist order that sees itself as threatened by chaos, turmoil, and sedition.

The return and revolts of the past

As we have already mentioned, the "Pinochet event" removed the layers of silence from memory, shaking the Concertación administrations from their pact of non-memory (forgetting the forgotten) due to the sudden explosion of news that surprised those who had covered up the ex-dictator's secret responsibility for crimes against humanity. The news of Pinochet's arrest obfuscated the Chilean Right's vindictive reaction – reviving the memory of Unidad Popular so as to continue condemning the supposed intrigues and plots of international Marxism. The daily newspaper *La Segunda*, which has the largest circulation of any national newspaper, took advantage of the "Pinochet event" by publishing the revision of certain portions of history performed by historian and ex-minister of the military regime Gonzalo Vial, which attempted to raise public awareness through a narrative based on a dogmatic opposition between Allende's destructive government and the reconstructive program installed by the military junta on September 11, 1973. Conveniently skipping over the parenthesis of the dictatorship that preceded the democratic transition, the Chilean Right embodied by Vial's historical vision tried to persuade society to see the past of Unidad Popular and the disastrous failure of Allende's government as a cautionary tale that should serve as an explanation for – and an exoneration of – the military coup.

Inspired by a dogmatic manipulation of the past, the Chilean Right used propaganda to convert the memory of Allende's government into a violent symbol of the nation's past, a distorted reference that served to reignite the hatred between political adversaries in a new, ideologically polarized episode (Pinochet's international arrest).

A hidden accumulation of memories of Unidad Popular arose again owing in large part to the activity of a new reactionary contingent of right-wing Chilean women. Among the many images loaded with historical and hysterical resonance were those shown on television of women in the streets defending Pinochet, demonstrating in much the same way they so vehemently did during the Unidad Popular era. The same nationalist fervor and military glorification of these groups of Pinochetista women inevitably recall Poder Femenino and the extreme right-wing militants of the Patria y Libertad [Homeland and Liberty] movement during the "March of Pots and Pans" that precipitated the overthrow of the Allende government in 1973.[2]

For a woman, to go out into the street and take ownership of it as a (masculine) territory of struggle and social action is to betray the mandate of bourgeois femininity that is traditionally kept within the privacy of the home and the family. Only the emergence of a political crisis (that of Unidad Popular), experienced with all the paroxysms of a dangerous and desperate situation, caused upper-class women to decide to betray gender roles and leave the intimacy of their homes. This kind of betrayal was always permitted on the condition that, once the danger was neutralized, the women would return to the conventions that reaffirm their confinement within the roles of wife and homemaker in the private sphere. Both in the years before the military coup and during the protests for Pinochet's release from European authorities, the women's uprising as a politically active force was based in the same call to defend the cohesion and stability of the nation (understood as a natural extension of the family) against all enemies.

Psychoanalysis – particularly in Julia Kristeva's reading, for example – discusses the difficulties that women experience in adhering to the social contract, in integrating themselves into the symbolic pact of discourse and identity that regulates the

relations between subjects and institutions. In certain circumstances, women project onto masculine power the paranoiac
counter-inauguration of the symbolic order they had initially
negated, thus transforming themselves into fanatic defenders
of the status quo – which is to say, they become the vigilant
protectors of the established patriarchal order. This explains
the compromises women have historically made with totali-
tarianism and authoritarianism: they submit in body and
soul to the forces of order that make up violent regimes and
eventually become the most fervent propagandists of those
regimes. When the values of order (continuity, stability,
harmony) are threatened by the chaotic figure of dis-order
(antagonisms, divisions, conflicts), which authoritarian and
totalitarian power associates with destruction and death,
women are called upon to embody the defense of life as a
value asserted by the ideology of motherhood as part of
their "natural" condition as the reproducers and saviors
of humankind. Life/death, order/chaos, integrity/dissolution:
these are the polarities that form a fertile scenario for the
intervention of the symbol of femininity that safeguards the
homogeneity of essences and the transcendent purity of the
categories of God, Homeland, and Family. The drifting of the
maternal-familiar toward the *national* is part of a patriarchal
and militaristic rhetoric that founds the nation on a supreme
good that self-sacrificing mothers must defend against the
anarchistic danger of revolution, thus saving the family
(traditions and conventions) from the disruptive signs used
by the forces of change to pervert the ideological and cultural
conformism of social normality. The figure of the internal or
external enemy, for all its threats to dissolve the purity of
the family and the nation, is accompanied by an unequivocal
demarcation between positive and negative values that serves
the guardians of order by imposing and maintaining its
inflexible dogma. Motivated by the international arrest of
Pinochet, the Chilean Right returned to indoctrination and
ideological reunification around the "national" in order to,
in their words, combat the effects of the new "malevolent
conspiracy" of international socialism and communism,
which they accused of having secretly organized Pinochet's
arrest and detention in London. Under the anti-communist
assumption that anyone who flies the red flag is detestable

because they have no country, no family, and no religion, the Pinochetista women of the Chilean Right declared war on these forces of evil (that is, the forces of international socialism and communism) for having dared to unjustly punish Pinochet, the "Savior of the Homeland."

Historically, we know that fascist discourse has played with women's desires, drives, and sexual fantasies (the virile sublimation of command, the eroticization of authority), basing itself on a family-oriented ideology that subordinates women to the state and the nation with stereotypes of mothers and wives who are obedient to the *Pater*, the leader of the family and the homeland. The televised scenes of Chilean women marching in the streets of Santiago and London in 1998 demonstrated how the protocols of religious authority, along with forms traditionally enshrined in popular religion in Chile, continued to determine the Pinochetista women's submissive veneration of military icons. We even witnessed the extremes of this Catholic veneration with the exhibition of a portable "Altar of the Homeland," complete with a small plaster statue that combined the faces of Pinochet and the Virgin Mary, conjugating within the same faithful rituality the Catholic imagery of the Marian cult and the patriotic *kitsch* of fervent militarism.

The slogan "Pinochet is immortal," which many of the protesters in Chile and London had written on their signs, fused this religious faith with the patriotic glorification of Pinochet's "modernizing work," thus postulating that through his immortalization this work would finally be reinvested with divine credit. Once it was blessed by faith, the work of the military government could aspire to last forever, reproducing in perpetuity Chile's neoliberal "miracle" of economic modernization. The religious fanaticism of Pinochet's female supporters re-absolutized him as a symbol in the Right's imaginary so as to reverse the fatal episode of the ex-dictator's fall from grace, reinvesting him with a transhistorical force. The deification of the human that took the figure of Pinochet from the too-contingent world of the knowledgeable present of his arrest and detention and transformed him into a supernatural icon evoked the "Pinochet is immortal" signs of the protests. It became obligatory for Pinochet supporters, who were so proud of his calculating and careful military strategy, to negate the sense of defeat they felt from seeing him mocked for his claims about the "malevolent conspiracy" of the international Left by forcefully invoking the timelessness and transcendence of myth. This is how the Pinochetista Right reinscribed the conjunctural incident-accident of Pinochet's arrest within the supercomputer code of destiny. Pinochet wrote a "Letter to Chileans" during his detention in December 1998, in which he fervently invokes God and Divine Providence and prays that the unfortunate sum of failures and mishaps that led to his humiliating international capture will forever be grandiloquently magnified because of the supreme figure of predestination that had made him into a martyr.[3]

Uproar in the streets

The televised images of the groups of Pinochetista women protesting in the streets made visible the social territoriality that restratified the power of money in the post-dictatorship city: a city where the unequal order that separates the rich from the poor is strictly maintained through municipal boundaries and architectonic cordons erected by real-estate speculation, isolating the "modernized" from the rest of the urban landscape and segregating waste and filth outside the unsullied perimeter of the zones of monetary accumulation and condensation where the wealthy live. The Pinochetista women protesting in the streets designated the most upscale district of Santiago, a residential neighborhood of embassies and corporate growth, as their reserved domain – that is, as the inviolable property of an economic class that exercises its superiority on the basis of the exclusive and excluding privilege of money.

During the military dictatorship, diplomatic neighborhoods such as this one had been sites of political asylum for those persecuted by Pinochet's military regime. Inverting this memory, the Pinochetista women decided to barricade themselves not inside but outside the British embassy, where they directed their poorly spoken, foul-mouthed, and fanatic cries and slogans. Shouts of "shitty communists!" – the same insults that upper-class women hurled at Allende supporters

during the Unidad Popular era – surged forth once again
from the lowest end of the spurious scale of distinction that
the Chilean bourgeoisie who live in these wealthy neighborhoods strive so hard to maintain. Foremost in the television
news coverage of the protest were contorted faces vomiting
out hatred, shouting "curses, profanities, and oaths … the
colloquialisms of the marketplace"[4] in a neighborhood that
explicitly lacks public plazas because it has been entirely
colonized by corporate power. The murderous violence of
this hatred revealed the cracks in the bourgeois composure
of these upper-class women, such that the vulgarity of their
detestable shouting caused the makeup of their obscene
masks to run.

The call to "Boycott English products!" endorsed by
political leaders of the Chilean Right (such as Evelyn Matthei)
as a response to Pinochet's international house arrest in
London revealed how these extremist defenders of neoliberalism saw the realm of consumption as the only frame of
reference and argumentation to which they could appeal.
The moral defense of the values and principles of Chilean
sovereignty that the Right attempted to invoke in response
to the purported offense to "national dignity" constituted by
Pinochet's arrest coexisted cynically in right-wing discourse
with the pragmatic calculus of a logic of commerce that
had replaced exchange with extortion ("Boycott English
products!").

The transnationalization of consumption, economic
globalization, national sovereignty, the internationalization
of justice, and the universality of human rights: the Pinochet
case flagrantly staged the double-edged paradox that traps
the Right in a web of contradictions that divides it between
the *national* (an already outdated system of historical, traditional, and religious references that still form the basis of
patriotic symbols as an identifying flag for the nation-state)
and the *post-national* (the global reconfiguration of societies
connected across the planet by the deterritorializing flows of
intensive capitalism). On the one hand, the Chilean Right
applauds the discourse of economic globalization that favors
the unfettered circulation of financial goods and values that
converge, in a utilitarian way, in the deals made by multi-
national conglomerates – as was planned all along by the

neoliberal model established in Chile by the Chicago School economists. On the other hand, this same Right anachronistically defends the benefits of inviolable borders, which they connect to national sovereignty, thus ethically rejecting what they applaud economically whenever this inviolability of borders finds itself threatened by the transgressive universalism of the discourse of human rights.[5] The Chilean Right that defends trade agreements and open borders only reacts against the dangers of globalization when it is asked to respect international law and to address the globalization of justice with regard to human rights. The Right seems not to have noticed that the counterpart of the capitalist expansion that subsumed Chile into the globalized integration of the world economy is the (for them, undesirable) obligation to adhere to international agreements about justice and the universal value of "human rights." With Pinochet's arrest, the Chilean Right found itself in an ideological and discursive contradiction between, on one side, its unrestricted defense of the model of free trade (that of an "open, outward-facing economy") led by transnational corporations that limitlessly expand the networks of the market society, and, on the other, a protectionism that seeks to take advantage of the legal assertion of the "territoriality of law" in order to continue covering up crimes that have still not been prosecuted in Chile by the national courts.

The multiple conflicts between opposing positions that, in connection with the words "internationality," "modernization," "right/law" ["derecho"], "universality," "sovereignty," and "territoriality," impacted interviews and public conversations about the Pinochet case show how these same words, whether enunciated by Pinochetista leaders or by human rights lawyers, are subject to appropriative and counter-appropriative operations of meaning that turn them into socio-communicative battlegrounds. Once again, terminological disputes turn into ideological arguments between the Right and the Left, which is to say, into conflicts over the right to name and to convert names into seals of legitimation of the truth of what one says. With regard to traumatic memories, we should recall that the words of memory are words that divide not only because of the opposition between the dictatorship's advocates and adversaries. They are also words that resound throughout the universe of Leftist sensibilities, where anyone who comes to control the system of official domination (saying, for example, "Transition" instead of "post-dictatorship") is confronted by the conquered of history: those who must fight to have their broken or crossed-out words recognized by the dominant narrative of memory as a valid "reconciliation" that has come to control memory and remove from it any biographical or subjective remainders of the catastrophe.

The war of images

Motivated by Pinochet's arrest, the streets of Santiago became the visual scene of a confrontation of violently clashing gestures. The image-memories of black-and-white photographs of the disappeared exhibited by the victims' families were engaged in a bitter war of truth against the photogenic simulations of Pinochet as a hero deployed by his defenders as a new symbolic offensive against the victims of the military dictatorship. The war between these Pinochet supporters and the families of the disappeared was ceaselessly produced in a language of photographic images. Groups of right-wing women displayed the emblems of the Pinochet cult: full-color posters of the Senator-for-Life, produced and airbrushed by advertising firms, were reproduced as stickers and t-shirts emblazoned with the slogan "I love Pinochet," with the word "love" represented by a heart (as seen on other promotional posters and stickers around the world that express affection for a city or a popular figure) in a graphic synthesis of language without borders that transnationalizes mass consumption and the tourism industry. For some reason, the partisan beneficiaries of the military regime's economic modernization chose to express their support for Pinochet in this code of commercial and touristic serialization of images that governs the felicitous becoming-commodity of signs in the era of intensive capitalism. In the most painful aspect of this promotional and touristic industrialization of consumers (logotypes and stereotypes) that live off the banality of series and *appearances*, one finds the women affiliated with the groups for the disappeared who demand truth and justice, which is to say, they demand the *appearance* of bodies that still have not been found.

The portraits of the disappeared displayed by their families are usually black-and-white photocopies, contemporary in a graphic sense with the revolutionary pamphlets that circulated during the militant period of the 1960s, a time before the modernization of politics that is today left to the media technologies of professional image-makers. The fading black-and-white photocopied portraits of disappeared political activists carried by the victims' families stand in contrast to the unabashed professional gloss of the Pinochet posters, bravely confronting the present technico-mediatization of the social with their technical pre-modernity. On the propaganda posters carried in the streets by his supporters, Pinochet smiles on the dictatorship's past and on the future of his agreed-upon liberation, thus appearing as the master of a photographic pose, defying eternity with impunity. Meanwhile, the photographs of the disappeared share the interval of hopelessness, submerged in the common grave of the neoliberal present because of all that the Transition has left unpublished: shattered biographies and wounded subjectivities, damaged bodies and broken affectivities. In the streets of Santiago, the victims' families marched with portraits of the disappeared and called on passersby to participate in the allegorical remains of a dissolved kinship ceremony. Torn from the pages of family albums, these unbound portraits accuse the "national" – the emblem of the Right and its defense of the "Chilean family" – of being nothing but a cruel simulacrum of unity and cohesion between mutually antagonistic components, based on an intractable judgment of the past that preserves this hostility.

At the opposite extreme of the unblemished surface of the image of a victorious, smiling Pinochet, adeptly attuned to the contemporary mediatization of politics, a battle was being waged by the opacity of grainy portraits whose material precariousness and disintegration betray the exhaustion of a story based on suppression and neglect, deferment and erasure. The grain of the photocopied black-and-white portraits of the disappeared reveals that these images are technically incapable of competing, in terms of clarity or brilliance, with the face of Pinochet, saturated by televisual chromatism. In fact, the Pinochet posters belong to the era of politics as image and spectacle promoted by the neoliberal Transition in which everything it *had too much of* (the gratifications of commodities and the promotional style of the new) was used to distract from what was *missing* (bodies and truth). The streets of Santiago activated this painfully asymmetric confrontation between the image-commodity (Pinochet as souvenir) and the memory-fetish (the portrait of the disappeared that, as a photocopy, itself gradually disappears). The exhaustion and melancholia of the visual past of a signifier-portrait in worn-out, photocopied black-and-white marked an insurmountable distance from the full-color images of the global hypercapitalism visually appropriated by Pinochet's defenders. While the Pinochetista family was reunited around the image of the ex-dictator, whose photogenic quality was the result of a cynical attempt to touch up the history of the dictatorship with the cosmetics of false martyrdom, the black-and-white ethics of the victims' faces – boldly facing forward and looking straight ahead – silently acted as a disturbing visual condemnation of the dissimulating and deceptive Pinochet, who was so blindly defended by his wealthy supporters.

3

Torments and Obscenities

There are difficult knots of signification between history and memory that are woven into the diffuse folds of twisted meanings. This tangled web of signs emerges out of the main story in the form of secondary narratives.

How can we revisit memory in such a way that the work of criticism can distance itself from the grand recompositions of the scene of sociopolitical analysis traced by a language without shadows or complexities? How can we disrupt the regular order of an untruthfully stable consensus on history and the past and address the babbling and zigzagging of memory? How can we respond to the confusion of those disarticulations of meaning that rebel against the pure and simple truth symbolized by homages to victimhood? Perhaps it is these most insidious fragments of a past shot through with impurities that we should re-read with precise attention to detail so that memory and remembrance may confess their knots of sin, anguish, and obscenity.

The autobiographies of Luz Arce and Marcia Alejandra Merino were published in the midst of the Transition, relating both women's stories, including their time as Leftist militants during the Unidad Popular regime and their subsequent arrest by the secret military police, the Dirección de Inteligencia Nacional [National Intelligence Directorate] (DINA), who imprisoned and tortured them until they agreed to become informers for the state for a period of more than ten years.[1]

Both women's stories intersect with various lines of difficult and tangled conflicts – ideological, moral, sexual, political, and ethical – which undoubtedly contributed to the utter lack of response of Chilean media to their publication. The press feigned ignorance of them, even though the information both books provided about the perpetrators of human rights violations directly interpellated the Transition and its institutional human rights policies. Arce's and Merino's testimonies adopted the autobiographical format of life stories that exhibit the verbal compulsion of a constant desire to say more, seemingly confirming the idea that "women don't know how to shut up."[2] It is as if this charge of verbal compulsion and its disobedient excess of words is how the public sphere was meant to punish them by marginalizing or disqualifying their stories. This excessive loquacity generally attributed to women would be, in the case of Arce and Merino, a serious infringement of the confidentiality rules about the secrets of imprisonment and torture – a subject about which the Transition has maintained a prudent discretion. Contrary to the commonplace according to which women talk incessantly without ever saying anything, Arce's and Merino's stories actually say far more than the words they use to tell those stories by combining an autobiographical rhetoric of sincerity with a tactics of the self through reconstructions of their lives that blur the lines between truth, moral amnesty, and published confession.

The blackmail of truth: bodies and names

Merino begins her autobiography by saying: "[B]etween the nakedness, the tremors caused by electric shocks, the humiliations, and the beatings, I uncontrollably shrieked out the first name: María Angélica Andreoli. I felt that everything was over for me. I had betrayed what I had loved most up to that moment."[3]

From the very beginning of her arrest and imprisonment, Merino was forced to tell the truth under the pressure of coercive methods. To speak the truth, to confess what she knew, was the condition that saved her body from torture, at the cost of only a few names. This autobiographical confession from Merino ("la Flaca Alejandra") seeks forgiveness for having betrayed certain names, and she does so by naming names again, this time in her autobiography, "to make known the names of those responsible and to provide background information that might help unmask them."[4] Her book concludes with an appendix in which she lists the names of the disappeared as well as the names of DINA officers, a roll-call of sorts that combines the primal scene of guilt (surrendering the names of the fatal victims of her betrayal) with its reverse (repentance) by facilitating the identification of perpetrators who have yet to be brought to justice. "La Flaca Alejandra" pays for her betrayal of militants by denouncing the hidden names of military agents in order to thereby compensate for the first crime and to pay her debt to society at the same time that she attempts to publicly rehabilitate herself. The book closes in an endless abyss that mechanistically "names names" in a compulsive alternation between the records of victims and perpetrators, placing the names of the victims and their torturers side-by-side in the same appendix, where they are all printed in capital letters, thus making them appear equal. However, if we move from the pages of the book to the sphere of mass media, we can verify that the effective social contract between victims and perpetrators is very different from what is postulated by this typographical equality of names in capital letters. In reality, victims and perpetrators do not possess the same ability to resonate with the public. Victims' voices continue to be silenced, while some of the main perpetrators attract all the public's attention due to the spectacular nature of their cases. Over several months (between June and October 1995), General Manuel Contreras – ex-head of the DINA and the main individual accused of human rights violations in Merino's autobiography – dominated national news coverage with an illegitimate and media-orchestrated illness intended to defer the beginning of his prison sentence, which he was to serve after finally having been convicted of murder.[5] Contreras's refusal to pay for his crimes was hypermediatized in order to hide the unresolved tension of the victims' families' legitimate desire to know the answer to the question

"Where are they?" – a question on which the press continued to remain silent. While Contreras was constantly in the news, as his stalling tactics became a means to avoid serving his sentence, the disappeared already knew the fate of being archived as mere pieces of evidence in the common grave of the official lists compiled by human rights commissions and tribunals. The comedic deferral of Contreras's sentence due to his alleged illness caught the public's attention once more with the hypertelevisual "*When?*" of his entrance into prison, thus sacrificing yet again the question "*Where?*" posed by the bodies that remained undocumented. This is the double national suspense (When will justice be served? When will the truth be known about what happened to the victims?) of one and the same story in a continuous present, with its strings secretly connected to a silent point in the Transition's official negotiations. Pulling on a single thread will cause the entire fabric to unravel because all its connections are invisibly welded by the complicity of silence that holds together the dark background of the well-kept secrets of a democracy that remains under the watchful eye of the military.

Obscenity I

During his stay in the military hospital in Talcahuano in 1995, Contreras was taken to different clinics to undergo the examinations that would confirm the ailments that would postpone the start of his prison sentence. Images of Contreras appeared a number of times on Chilean television, showing the general as reduced to a patient waiting to be examined. Astonishingly, these images placed him in a relation of formal analogy with the bodies of the victims whose torture he had cruelly ordered: the same compulsory movement from one facility to the next, being ordered to undress and to assume specific positions, to be subject to the fragmenting action of machines that damage the body in the search for a truth that will serve as either a confession or a diagnosis.

Theatrically performing his illnesses, Contreras necessarily found himself in the unenviable position of a horizontal body disposed to manipulation against its will, after having always practiced terror from the upright (vertical) position of command: he was now a body laid out as a patient, at the mercy of the television camera's examining eye that anatomically reduced him in order to bring secret information to light.

Contreras was parodically condemned by television to be the victim of some of the same corporeal technologies of truth with which his detainees were cruelly abused: submission to observation, being made the focus of medical interrogation, being surveilled by the machinery of examination, being reduced to the object of one's physical condition. The media coverage of Contreras's illness ultimately took on the character of a symbolic revenge in the imaginary of anyone who identified with his victims.

Images of Contreras's medical procedures broadcast on radio and television revealed the organic and visceral details of tissues invaded by colon cancer, subjecting his poor health to the investigative transparency of close-up shots of the internal and morbid depths of semi-shameful areas of his body that were obscenely penetrated by the news media. Contreras's unhealthy body was figuratively submitted to an entire array of semantic associations that link the imaginary of cancerous diseases to the pathological figures of suspicious and malignant individuals, causing these associations to be inevitably transferred from the body (the zone of abnormal proliferation) to the mind (the creator of indignity and monstrosity). The diabolically resonant echo of the expression "against nature" that was applied to Contreras's intestinal movements and repeated as such by the entire national press indirectly communicated to citizens the latent subtext of an expected moral judgment. The expression "contra natura" (formulated through medical diagnosis) reconfirmed Contreras's inhumanity as a subject. The literal bodily symptom made it possible to use the term "degeneration" in a figurative way as an ethical condemnation of a degenerate former military leader.

Perpetual betrayal

In their autobiographies, Arce and Merino designate themselves as "Luc Arce, informer and traitor," and "la

Flaca Alejandra, collaborator." Both narratives tell us that
their first acts of betrayal were giving up information under
torture, out of the fear of pain. There was a dividing line that
marked giving up "the first name" and separated the zone of
loyalty, in which one is still *whole*, from the zone of betrayal,
in which one ends up informing on one's comrades because
one's (moral and psychical) integrity has finally been *broken*.
The first betrayal violates the moral principle of conviction
and its ideal of uprightness in which loyalty is connected to
integrity, while at the opposite extreme of betrayal this ideal
is destroyed. However, as we make our way through Arce's
and Merino's autobiographies, this straight line of sharp
separation between the (pure) "before" and the (impure)
"after" of the first offense is also "broken": it ambiguously
doubles and ramifies. What are the first confessions and
betrayals that turned Arce and Merino into traitors? Giving
up the first name under torture, or later becoming DINA
officers in exchange for the promise of freedom, or their
subsequent efforts to be accepted and recognized by the
hierarchy of military power? The very contours that delineate
the profile of betrayal are themselves treacherous. One never
quite knows how reliable the supposedly remorseful language
on display in these autobiographies is, or at what undefinable
margins of the story the testimonial truths of repentance start
to disintegrate. The figure of these authors' betrayal does
not have a clear design but rather exceeds boundaries that
are erased and then redrawn in regions of knowledge and
judgment that are crisscrossed with doubts and uncertainties.
In pardoning their betrayal, are we not betraying the memory
of those who died because they were themselves betrayed by
these now-confessed authors? Can we definitively trust that
this published truth is the whole truth if the authors themselves
admit that, invoking legal prudence, they have many times
only confessed "half-truths" in order "to protect other
involved third parties"? Furthermore, we cannot lose sight
of the fact that Arce's and Merino's autobiographies, which
demand forgiveness for the confession of betrayal, distract
our attention from other less well-known (but more collectively mute, more nationally insidious) betrayals. The symbol
of betrayal extends over the Transition, ramifying itself into
similar figures which then multiply incredulity and distrust.

The reemergence of suspicion brought about by these two autobiographies generalizes the effect of perpetual betrayal in which the Transition is imprisoned. Although the Transition's official slogan has been transparency (of processes, language, and actions intended to hide nothing and expose everything), these two books helped to promulgate the feeling that the division between the private (the secret) and the public (the confessable) covertly inhabits the interior of democratic officialdom itself, filling its institutional hallways with secret orders, restricted materials, and official agreements between indirect powers. From lies to cover-ups, from disloyalty to perjury: the figures of deception and betrayal reveal to us the multiple cracks within the hidden pact that connects certain names in the Transition government to the unconfessable secrets of the dictatorship, still shrouded in anonymity. Arce's and Merino's books extend the shadows of doubt over calls for "transparency," making it seem as if such calls are simply responding to a politics of the image meant to obfuscate the manipulation of their traitorous cooperation with the state.

Obscenity II

In Carmen Castillo's video La Flaca Alejandra *(1994), Alicia Barrios, ex-militant of the MIR (Movimiento de Izquierda Revolucionaria [Leftist Revolutionary Movement]), does not care to play the game of truth that torments the protagonist, Marcia Alejandra Merino. Barrios is a woman who, in a certain way, mocks the pathos of Merino's confession, which she uses as an attempt to justify her demand for forgiveness, her moral superiority supported by the pain of having known at first hand the hell of torture, offering the excuse of physical weakness as the cause of her inability to withstand the violence she endured. In Castillo's video, Barrios says she does not believe Merino's story and, almost as if she finds it amusing, laughs at the pathetic tone of the conversation between Merino and Castillo, immersed as they both are in the shared dilemmas of memory and forgiveness. Castillo's voiceover comments on Barrios's appearance in the video, telling us that this is a woman who disguises herself every Saturday to "act out the artifice of a country that dissimulates, lies, and cheats. She provokes the end of the farce according to which 'nothing happens here.'" Barrios is portrayed as a comical figure who turns to acting and disguise in her carnivalesque game of masks and lies. This game of artifices, alluded to by Barrios's appearance in Castillo's video, offers a metaphorical key to understanding a certain deceptiveness in the world of the Transition.*

Lies, deceit, and betrayal; artifice and disguise; simulation and dissimulation. Every day we witness an entire series of pretenses carried out by various Transition officials who opportunistically switch up discourses and behaviors to align with the "politics of change" that they use to justify their constantly shifting identities. Between ruin and celebration, between funeral procession and carnival of masks, various individuals associated with the Transition have exchanged mourning for entertainment. On display in the society pages of the Chilean paper of record, El Mercurio, we can see to what extent the old codes of honor and morality of Leftist militancy have been replaced by the narcissistic script of social imagination.

The Transition's family photo album is full of false poses and untruthful declarations: a game of appearances designed to compensate for the breakdown of political meaning on the Left with an exhibitionist proliferation of attractive signifiers promoted in a media-saturated present still controlled by the right-wing press. It is as if the Transition obscured the theme of disappearance (tragically modulated by those stricken by grief) with the frivolous register of appearance (the market of styles and the commercialization of the pose).

Conversion

Merino's and Arce's autobiographies take the form of *confessions* in which guilt and remorse constitute the framework of a narrative of atonement. Both autobiographies portray the progressive continuity of the course of life written in the mnemonics of remembrance that orders the past in a linear, reconstitutive sequence of facts and explanations. Both autobiographies open with preliminary statements signed by their authors which declare and summarize the contents of their confessions, superimposing the point of arrival – the chronological end of the life-trajectory recreated in the book – onto the point of departure: the beginning of the story. This overlapping of the beginning and the end, hardly unusual in autobiographical writing, recapitulates the facts contained in the book, causing them to appear as if they were signed by a subject-author who coincides with herself: a subject-author who uses the narrative as a means to reunite, within a coherent matrix of identity, with her own origin. This effect of identitarian reintegration is achieved through the story's circularity, which narratively circumvents the "I," covering the gaps of any factual inconsistencies with a sustained and continuous line. In the cases of Merino and Arce, it is as if the surviving word that narrates torture requires a sense of finality in its story which promises the editorial closure of testimony, a definitive suture of the still-open wounds of memory and meaning.

However, in addition to being confessions, both autobiographies are also *conversions*: they describe the moral transformation their authors underwent, beginning with their reencounter with God, which taught them to take responsibility for their sins and gave them "the courage to tell the whole truth" in seeking forgiveness.

The rules of performativity of the confession-conversion genre tell us that the subject's word acts out the experience it describes with no further proof of the truth (that it *says* the truth) than what is revealed by the speaker's own subjective testimony. It is an internal consciousness that dictates the private truth of the confession-conversion, and that truth has no verifiable referent outside the biographical intimacy of the personal narrative being put into words. There is always something morally disturbing in the unverifiability of a confession's sincerity. Merino's and Arce's autobiographies are troubled by this moral disturbance that emerges from the unverifiable condition of confession. However, in both books the effect of this disruption of belief in "the truth" appears to be symbolically regulated and controlled by a religious guarantee (God, the Church, etc.), invoked as support for the sincerity of their repentance. Arce's *El infierno* [Hell] includes a prologue written by a priest who testifies to her conversion to the Catholic faith. This prologue also offers us the merciful example of Christian forgiveness as a model that attempts from the very beginning of the book to anticipate and secure our future forgiveness as readers. The undecidability of the truth content that usually characterizes confession narratives is negated here by a prologue written from the perspective of a moral authority who has clearly taken the side of the confessor. It is as if the priestly voice of this exemplary prologue was meant to relieve readers from exercising their faculty of judgment and thus submit the process of the adjudication of truth to the hierarchy of an ecclesiastical voice that predetermines the readers' reception of the text as a model of Christian exemplarity. By editorially meddling in the moral secret of these political confessions in order to testify to their veracity, the Church of the Transition reveals there is no doubt that it still dictates the standards for values and behaviors in matters of public credibility.

The converts' narratives of their dignifying reencounters with God bring about several other moralizing reunions that end up ordering their life trajectories. For example, the description Arce gives of her conversion in *El infierno* shows how she passes from the code of political militancy to the rite of observance, from political dogma to religious creed. The imperative of duty shifts between the first and second parts of the book by exchanging political ideology for Christian religion, but it is in either case the same fidelity to a superior and absolute Truth that subjects Arce's identity to a severe framework of invocations and prescriptions ("so often without faith, the miserable Luz began to wish to say 'yes' to the Lord").[6] Throughout both books, the reiteration of obedience to a vertical system of doctrines and commands only reinforces the generic-sexual convention of submissive, loyal, and docile femininity. This convention is formalized by realigning the sign *woman* with the traditional roles proscribed by social morality: "Father Gerardo ... showed me God in this world. To him I owe learning how to value family, motherhood, commitments, etc."[7] The transformative value of religious conversion through faith saves the political traitor from the weight of her sins by calling her conscience to a reencounter with the Truth. To complete this itinerary, she must go through the symbolic tribute of another (gendered) reencounter with her nature as a woman: a sexual nature that reduces her to her vocation as wife and mother. This double reconciliation with the Truth and the Family combines the happy ending of a return to the straight and narrow path of good conduct for those women who had betrayed not only the political ideals of the Leftist resistance (by acting as informers) but also this idealized notion of femininity by having dedicated their bodies and souls to political militancy.[8] Both women now return to the fixed and established truths/ essences of a normative femininity regulated by the institution of the Family. The reintegration of the "traitors" into conventions of identity that welcome them back after they had strayed from the truth of their sense of self is sealed in both books through a familial and domestic reprogramming of the feminine condition that ultimately leads both to embrace the primordial roles of mother and wife. How else could it be in the Chilean Transition, where the dominating voice of the Church and Catholic traditionalism governs the sphere of social discourse and sanctions the politics of the body? The moralizing reconversions recounted in Arce's and Merino's autobiographies return their authors to the dogma of faith as well as to conventional gender norms. Without this ideological and sexual recompense, demanded by the Christian-familial norm, the journey of repentance encapsulated in these two political autobiographies would be seen as incomplete – imperfect – by the Church and society. It is only through the contrition of the sexual bodies that testify to both women's religious conversion that their lives as women can be read as healthy examples of reintegration (in terms of identity and gender) according to the moral conventions of Chilean society during the Transition.

Silence, screams, and the printed word

The autobiographies of Arce and Merino come back repeatedly to questions of naming, voice, and identity, going through a stigmatizing sequence of debilitations, confiscations, and annulments of the self that, after having been reduced through the sacrifice of the person, seeks its ultimate compensation in the indelibility of the word (the text) *and* the signature (the name of the author on the cover).

First, their militant pasts required both women to resort to using pseudonyms to obscure and disguise their dangerous, clandestine identities. Then, during their incarceration they were stripped of their "legal existence" and were reduced to "a simple number" in military prisons. Afterward, their connections to military intelligence operatives (DINA-CNI) made it so they often had to change their names in order to hide their tracks and to confound any attempt to identify them. Suppressed or distorted identities left gaps of alienation and lack in the subjects of this double story of someone who perceives herself as a *not-I*: someone with "an usurped name" and "an existence without identity."[9] The fractured coherence of this "someone" is even greater when it has passed through the physical test of torture, which disarticulates and reduces the person to a mere "something," just lying there, to be used until it dies.

Silence (the tenacious refusal to utter any sound) and screaming (the disfiguration of speech) are two expressions of torture that defy the laws of the phonetic articulation of sound. Silence and screaming are what precede and exceed the pronunciation of the "first name," which, when betrayed under torture, temporarily suspends the punishments inflicted on the torture victim's body. Silence and screaming are two forms of non-speech – that is, they are two unusable manifestations of the word whose resistance must be forcefully converted by the torturer into usable words with meaning.[10] The *spoken* confession is the victorious trophy of the confrontation between, on one side, a damaged and useless body and, on the other, an apparatus of cruelty that has finally ripped a useful word out of the torture victim. The physical violence of torture literally breaks its victims. It fractures the corporeal unity of the person, dislocating their limbs. It detonates the core of conscious reasoning. After the suffering of torture reduces the body to a pre-linguistic state of silence or to the extra-linguistic state of screaming, it is written testimony that will allow the destroyed subject to verbalize her story and thus to overcome the destructive limit to which she was subjected. Allowing the subject to name the unnamable and to do so with the written word, written testimony avenges the inhumane past of the victims' abject silence and screaming.

Arce repeatedly associates the blocking of identity with the trauma of the loss of speech: "it was as if my voice made no sound at all; as if it did not even exist."[11] The lack of voice, of voice as an expressive vehicle of the speaking subject, externally expresses the destruction of a person who has been converted by the limit experience of torture into someone now incapable of uttering a sound, of testifying to herself as a source of meaning. After so much deterioration of the faculty of speech, to write a book, to turn to the eloquence of playing with the art of words, could be for these two ex-torture victims a superlative way to *recover their voices* as authors of their own stories. Their published testimonies are the tangible evidence that they finally "found the words" that were so often unavailable in the past to transmit the meaning of the horror through which they lived.

Before publishing their autobiographies, Arce and Merino had already broken the silence that weighed heavily on their pasts as DINA informers and collaborators when they went to testify in court and offer their confessions to help clarify the truth in cases of human rights violations. Their autobiographies thus exhibit the subsequent (added) condition of being a textual supplement to these earlier court statements. Why was it necessary to write a book that functions as a supplement to a previously attested truth which has already fulfilled its socially useful function as material evidence? It seems that the media interviews and court statements that surrounded Arce's and Merino's first public confessions were not enough to have their identities (which had long ago been captured and imprisoned by repressive blackmail) returned to them. It was as if both women needed their testimonies to be published as autobiographies in order to fully repossess themselves. It seems that the publication of the recollection of the self, shattered by life, through a story in the form of a book was capable of retrospectively granting verbal force and narrative continuity to everything that had been previously smashed to pieces.

The autobiographical pact formally guarantees the concordance of the narrator, author, and character, sealing the question of identity under the reaffirmative mark of a triple emphasis on the "I." The autobiographical pact and its reaffirmation-confirmation of identity project onto the torture victims the illusion of being able to repair the damage of the multiple annihilations of the self they suffered throughout a long succession of violences. Assuming the referential and biographical continuity of the subject, testimony and its autobiographical conventions fill in the gaps left by the suppression and alienation of identity. Furthermore, the criterion of veracity that sustains the definition of testimony based on rules of the authenticity of speech provide convincing evidence of a reality that reverses the insistent "fear of not being believed" that both authors manifest throughout their narratives.

The testimonial recomposition of the "I" that supports both autobiographies is guided by a will to recover one's name: *El infierno* begins with the sentence "My name is Luz Arce, and it has been very costly for me to recover this name," while *Mi verdad* [My truth] ends with "I, Marcia Alejandra Merino ... ." Both women's names were so often obliterated and distorted that today they must be pronounced out loud and written in capital letters to conjure the ghosts of identity disfiguration that inhabit their clandestine and traitorous past. The capital letters on the covers of both books lift up the shame of guilt and publicly account for a finally reconstructed identity that dares to say "I," patenting its own truth under the legitimizing authority of an editorially validated, printed publication. In fact, *El infierno* describes how Arce went from "an usurped name" to a legitimate and legitimated name (a proper name) after having been doubly endorsed by a guarantee of moral (the Church) and political (her ex-comrades from her period of militancy – now bureaucrats in the Concertación government – whom she asked for forgiveness) recognition.

If the *signature* is a sign that identifies what is most *proper* to a person, if Arce's story is a story of the deappropriations of the "I," what better than the author's signature to consecrate the reappropriation of a name that had been previously *expropriated* as the trophy of an identity that is finally discernible once again?

The author's signature is the editorial mark that confirms the propriety of meaning. It is also the emblem of an identity that owns its brand, that circulates its name like a designatable, referable, and citable sign in the cultural market of authors' names. The name written in capital letters in the prestigious place of the author's signature (featured on the cover of the Editorial Planeta edition of the book) concludes the process of the reappropriation of the self in Arce's autobiography: "I knew that living in Chile had its price. *And that price was to publicly declare that my name is Luz Arce.*"[12] In this case, the author's recorded signature also materializes a certain symbolic economy of reconciliation because it allows the collaborator-traitor to be recognized (through the publication of her autobiography) as forgiven by the cultural market of the Transition, which was willing to convert her testimony into a published commodity. The publisher's legitimizing and valorizing brand, after so much contempt, finally gives the traitor's name a *price* on the market of social representation. However, who is the target audience for these two books? Who will benefit from the circulation of this price/prize of publication in the Chilean Transition, which has, through forgetting and an unwillingness to remember, systematically negated the voices of those who were tortured?

Memory and market

Published in 1993 and 1994 respectively, Arce's *El infierno* and Merino's *Mi verdad*, which combine biographical confession and political testimony, were neither discussed nor analyzed in terms of the obscure meanderings of the truths they contain according to the script of guilt and repentance.

The exquisitely printed pages of *El infierno*, which sought to capture everyone's eye in the stalls at the Chilean Book Fair, right in the middle of Santiago, did not elicit any reaction. It is as if the truth to which Arce bears witness in her recollection of the dark past of the dictatorship were simply one truth among many others, as worthy of consideration or disregard as all the rest. Although they contradict one another, truths about the past all seem to be easily reconcilable because they fit into a pluralistic diversity which applauds in all testimonies the individual particularity of a story that seems to want to absolve society from the general responsibility of collective reading. Thus, the "memory boom" (Andreas Huyssen) promoted by the confessional market avoids the confrontation between the discursive strategies through which each construction of memory chooses to differentiate and even oppose itself to other memories.

El infierno edits a fragment of the dictatorship that the Transition government published and circulated through one of the registered trademarks of its culture industry: Editorial Planeta. This fragment of memory enters the procession of a cultural market whose ideologically, aesthetically, and politically valorizing relativism cancels out its discrepancies. The speed of the circulation of commodities is due to the transitoriness with which it satisfies the drive for novelty stimulated by the substitutive rules of change and renewal. The dictatorship memoir circulated by the market enters this game of rapidly recycled signs that do not bother to give history more than a brief, passing mention: a hastily inserted reference that is designed not to upset the shallow rhythm of the variations and diversions of media aesthetics with an inopportune demand for information that would, with the seriousness of its meaning, require an ethical judgment on issues of conscience from opposing sides. The marketplace and television have expelled from their accelerated rhythms of consumption anything that requires a delay of attention (and intellection), which is no longer compatible with the simultaneity of the purely visual effects of technological screens.

Obscenity III

The image of "Guatón [Fatso] Romo" (Osvaldo Romo, one of the cruelest DINA torturers) being interviewed on Chilean television in June 1995 and commenting on the dark details of how he carried out state terrorism, was obscene in numerous ways. The broadcast of the interview abused the delicacy of certain fragile limits of emotional resistance that once again violated the still-persecuted victims of the military coup. Romo's televised interview was like a blow to the scarred memory of an all too wounded past, it abused the shattered affectivities of irreparably damaged lives. Nevertheless, the interview with Romo failed to produce within collective sensibility even the slightest disruption of the norm. There was no public complaint about the untenable violation of memory produced by this story of unpunished evil, which we were all forced to witness as a captive television audience. Nor did anyone complain about the nonexistent borders of ethical gatekeeping that suddenly brought us face-to-face with the worst: the brazen reappearance of a vicious murderer who, enjoying the undignified privilege of a television interview, usurped the victims' place of public enunciation in favor of those whom the Chilean press refused to put on trial in the media.

The obscenity of this interview was related to Romo's own account but also to the realization that the ethically shocking aspects of the interview did not in any way disrupt the smooth and polished visual continuity of the information-advertising-entertainment of Chilean television. The prevailing sense was that the limits between the demonstrable and the indemonstrable had been abolished by the neutral permissiveness of indifference, which absorbs and recycles everything in deft operations that empty out all content.

Even if the interview did not reveal any previously unknown horror, the vicious exhibitionism of "Guatón Romo" – who defiantly related these horrors in terms of absolute hatred – personalized the sinister impunity that permeates the Transition's media networks. We were forced to endure this ex-torturer's monstrously unscathed image, protected from all physical punishment by the abstract (incorporeal) distance of the television screen, which not only kept him safe but also garnered fantastic ratings for the news program.

Broadcast on another network during the same week of June 1995, the program Mea Culpa *recreated the scene of a crime that was perpetrated by the repressive apparatus of the military regime. Its reality-show-style gruesomeness provoked a more polemical response than Romo's horrifying interview. It is as if the recorded reality of the latter interview were a less spectacular document than that offered by* Mea Culpa *as a genre program (reality television) that has met with success precisely for the way in which it (melodramatically) blurs the lines between reality, realism, and simulation.* Mea Culpa *is a program that not only takes advantage of this confusion but also accompanies its most dubious scenes with a journalistic locutionary performance: the muddled sentimentality and the viscous pathos of a "drama of conscience" translated into melodrama. In comparison to the illusory performance of reconstructed scenes (on which the success of the televisual genre of* Mea Culpa-*style testimony is based), it seems that the interview with Romo lacked the deceptive, doubling supplement of "recreation" that would have given it the same polemical impact as the reality show. Perhaps only in this way, with the help of doubling and recreation, would the disgusting contents of this interview have more deeply and dramatically conveyed a commensurate sense of horror.*

The obscenity of Mea Culpa *consists in the repulsive, moralizing commentary that disguises the gruesome benefits of the televisual trade in simulacral emotions. The obscenity of Romo's presence on the screen had to do with the absence of any critical commentary willing to openly discuss the scandal of how the rules of modesty-truth-morality that govern our daily condition as television viewers are constructed to censor minor transgressions (and to commercialize the censorship of its inoffensive sexual aspect) with the purpose of systematically diverting our attention from the offenses of the shameless appearance on TV of torturers like Conteras, Romo, and others.*

4

Confessions of a Torturer and His (Abusive) Journalistic Assemblage

In the post-dictatorship era, one primary ethical responsibility is to oppose the forces of oblivion that rapidly seek to dissolve the traumatic bonds of a historically convulsive past in the trivial, remainderless superficiality of the neoliberal present. However, there is a second critical responsibility that obliges us to rigorously mistrust the recycling of the industrialized boom market of memory. We should practice a vigilant counter-interpretation of the various artifacts of memory that attempt to rescue the victims' past, but we should also remember that this counter-interpretation risks betraying the memory of their suffering by allowing it to become trivialized through an inappropriate, "everyday" language or through the crudeness of oversimplified voices.

I invoke this critical responsibility with regard to the book _Romo: confesiones de un torurador_ [Romo: Confessions of a Torturer] (2001), written by the journalist Nancy Guzmán.[1] Gauging the value of a book like this one is a difficult and uncomfortable task. On the one hand, we might all concur that its publication effectively fulfills one of the book's self-proclaimed purposes – to account for the obscure aspect of the truth of how torture was carried out in military detention centers through the detailed account of one of its primary and most active practitioners: Osvaldo Romo. By revealing all that was suffered and insufferable, Guzmán's book purports to help keep alive that wounding remembrance, to prevent its image from losing intensity so that the memory of these abuses may not be weakened in spite of the machinery of impunity's desire to erase it.[2] The monstrous image of Romo portrayed in this book might serve, with its sinister deformities and defects, to "lay bare the horror, the ugliness, the filth that our society keeps in the recesses of its history,"[3] which is to say, to exhibit the abominable so that the abominations of memory will unsettle the false normality of the official memory of the Transition government, which is overly confident about its capacity for reconciliation. Seen in this way, perhaps it makes sense that the book was awarded the Premio Planeta for Investigative Journalism in recognition of its contribution to memory.

However, on the other hand, no sooner do we begin examining the construction of the book itself (in order to closely follow the performance of signs that serves as the narrative and setting of the accounts of torture) than we find baleful errors in the ways in which words are tied together, statements are connected, images are overlapped, and scenes and sequences are assembled. These mistakes and blunders cause certain parts of the book to grossly disregard all moral prudence in exhibiting a depraved fragment of the murderous memory of Romo, who, unfortunately, manages to emerge triumphant and unscathed from the publication of his ghoulish reconstruction. Considering the apparent inconsistency and incompetency of the book's composition (which also violates several ethical boundaries), the decision to give Guzmán an award for investigative journalism comes across as either ignorant or negligent.

By dismantling the assemblages of meaning that make up the story related by Guzmán's interview with Romo, there emerges an unreflective thread of fatal slips, unpardonable failures, and illicit associations between words and images that bring the torture victims' past into a confrontation with the torturer's present through an obscene reconstruction of history that erases the temporalities of yesterday and today in a dissolving repetition. This unnoticed fading of repetition results in a failure of the disassociation between past and present that plays such a strategic role for the victims, thus causing them to separate themselves from the traumatic experience of torture and to relocate their experiences to another, different, scene of the reconfiguration of the past.[4]

To exercise our critical responsibility with regard to the victims' memories we must denounce the way in which certain games of signs, whether due to negligence or tactlessness, open up the old wounds of damaged subjectivities. In spite of the well-intentioned desire to recover the victims' memories in order to save them from social oblivion (and there is no doubt that this was Guzmán's guiding intention), certain careless admissions of memory unintentionally reproduce a violence of meaning that, due to the vulgarity of failed words, ends up indulging in the journalistic expediency of feeding on morbidity.

The scene of the interview

The book's title, *Romo: confesiones de un torturador*, commits its first mistake by disguising the "interview" of which the book consists, calling it instead a "confession." The confession "is not only one of the many language games that rules our social being; it also decisively establishes its legitimacy in the ethical space of truth-telling: to confess is to bring a hidden truth into the present, a sin that demands expiation, and it is also (in its Christian version) to express repentance, assuming the promise of 'never again.'"[5] Both the act of confessing and the genre of confession are either implicitly or explicitly plotted out, motivated by the desire to reveal the secret of a behavioral infraction that, in seeking forgiveness, is narrated under the sign of the self-consciousness of evil. Romo's attitude in the book mocks the rigor of this demand for truth and repentance borne by the established definition of the confessional genre. On the book's back cover, we read the following fragment from Romo's text: "*You can say that I tortured, okay, that much is true and it was a good thing.* But you cannot say I was a scoundrel. You can say, right, that I fulfilled a phase and carried it out very well. My conscience is clean. *I think I would do it all again.*"[6] While the book's front cover and the genre of "confession" with which it identifies promise a sincere willingness on the part of the speaker to engage in confession-conversion, the description

on the back cover cynically undermines the moral expectations generated by the declaration of the title. The front and
back covers function as the recto and verso of the publishing
industry's game of deception and disillusionment. While the
front cover leads us to believe that, according to the rhetoric
of confession, the person named in the title is going to face
the consequences of his actions (to lay bare a hidden truth
and to express his remorse for what he has done), the back
cover allows the torturer's inflammatory speech to close the
book with a demonstration of shamelessness that manages to
occupy with impunity the privileged place of someone who,
now finished with the publication of history, still has *the
last word*. Why has the back cover been dedicated entirely
to Romo's appalling conclusion, thus giving him the luxury
of closing or not closing the story of torture, of maintaining
horror in the present with this sinister verbal threat: *"I think
I would do it all again"*? Without the prosecuting power of a
decisive response that would strip Romo of his indecent right
to the last word, Guzmán's book allows him to impose on
society at large its intolerable and inconclusive ending, which
consists of a new, suspended threat. Why has this privilege
been granted to Romo's disgusting statement, which he uses
to promote himself, on the cover of the book? Is it a matter of
trust in the market's indifference to memory or, even worse,
is it a matter of collusion with its most obscene resources?
The fact is, the memory market is able to tolerate certain
criminal deformities that attract readers' curiosity when they
are promoted as the exaggerated manifestation of an unusual
case (like, for example, Romo's) which bursts forth in an
abscess of individual madness in order to obscure with this
supposed abnormality the true systematicity of the apparatuses that made this madness so brutally efficient.

Guzmán explains her reasons for wanting to interview
Romo: "[H]opeful about the possibility of meeting the
Chilean Scilingo, I decided to go to see him, thinking that
he might have similar reasons for his actions: Romo was
the only one arrested for human rights violations, he was
abandoned and put on trial for following orders."[7] Stated
with such brusqueness and without any consistent mark of
critical reflection that would make her investigative orientation more precise, the prevailing sense is that Guzmán's

principal objective was to engage in journalistic competition and to break a story comparable to that of Scilingo's
shocking live testimony on Argentine television.

The sense that Guzmán is concerned more than anything
else with procuring shocking material that will make the book
a media sensation is reinforced by various passages that inter-
nally circulate around the sensationalism of the unexpected:
"It will be *the first and only time* that a torturer will speak on
camera to explain, without a shred of modesty, a small part
of the suffering of the women, men, and children who passed
through the torture centers of the Chilean dictatorship"; or,
"It was not possible for me to accept no for an answer, *to
lose this opportunity to expose the barbarism of torture, on
camera, as related by its most notorious practitioner.*"[8]

Media success (Romo's televised interview, which,
according to Guzmán, was to be internationally broadcast
on a program called *Primer impacto*) and the publishing
boom (the book's status as a best seller) are tacitly confused
in the cross-references that predetermine the text's horizon
for massive and rapid consumption. Guzmán says to Romo:
"If you grant me this interview, I can get the attention of the
300 million people who make up the Spanish-speaking world
from Canada to Tierra del Fuego"; at the same time, she
invites the reader to share in asking the question: "Why is this
book being published now, five years after Romo's televised
interview (which shocked the nation and the entire continent)
aired on North American television, a time when the book
might have been a best seller?"[9] *Romo: confesiones de un
torturador* thus combines the public [*lo público*] (the televised
shop window through which the interview was broadcast)
with the audience [*el público*] (the masses of readers capti-
vated by the Sunday rankings in which the newspaper *El
Mercurio* rates newly published titles) in one and the same
advertising gesture. It is as if Guzmán had confused the
public [*lo público*], the audience [*el público*], and the realm of
advertising [*lo publicitario*] in order to thus satisfy the instantaneous rhythm of up-to-the-minute news by defying the need
for a reflexive prudence that might help carefully unknot the
historical complexity of traumatic memory.

When Guzmán interviewed him, Romo was writing his
memoirs: "I am writing my book. I am writing because

in my book are all the things that I saw, achieved, and made throughout my life."[10] Romo, Guzmán tells us, had agreed to give her the interview because he was tempted by her promise that the publicity generated by the television broadcast of his testimony from prison would result in massive sales for his future book ("Even if only 10 percent of the viewers are interested in your story, you already have thirty million books sold").[11] Although Guzmán justifies her appeal to Romo's desire for publishing fame as a demonstration of professional ingenuity designed to counter his anticipated refusal to be interviewed, what comes through most clearly is this artifice of seduction via the promise of media popularity as the primary agreement between one person pursuing an "exclusive interview" and another who, during their conversation, remarks, "This interview is going to make you famous."[12] This first chain of *advertising-publicity-publication*, which unites the interviewer and the interviewee around the desire for the circulation of words as both bargaining chip and seduction, also subjects both the ex-torturer and the journalist to the exhibitive value of memory as a communicational commodity that can attain massive success. What could be more pleasing to someone like Romo, whose "constant exhibitionism" made it so "all of the detainees could clearly identify him because he liked to introduce himself to them so that they could see him and *know his name*,"[13] than to see the publication of this interview disguised as confession and memoir (since confession and memoir are genres that revolve around the desire for the inscription of the author-protagonist's proper name on the cover of a book)?

Guzmán's book reconstructs the itinerary of her preparation for the television interview with Romo, which was broadcast on May 18, 1995 by the North American Spanish-language network Univisión and gives an account of their various pre-recording sessions in the Santiago Penitentiary. From chapter to chapter the book also intersperses investigative materials associated with cases of human rights violations affecting people whose names are mentioned in Romo's account. Journalistically speaking, Guzmán could have achieved the goal of revealing the entire terrible truth of "the secrets of torture that Chile and the world must know," using the interview with Romo to obtain and communicate newsworthy information without necessarily revealing the methods used in the preparation of the book. There are multiple techniques for arranging and editing the material recorded during an interview that would allow its transcription to achieve the end of placing a hidden truth before the public while also guaranteeing its veracity without the interview's own apparatus becoming too obviously visible in the resulting book. Guzmán opts instead to describe every stage of her interview with Romo exactly as it happened and uses this information as a deliberate form of recreating and showing the *live and direct* shared situation of the interviewer and her interviewee.

As we know, the interview is a conversational genre with dialogical format implying the existence of a "you" and an "I" that mutually recognize and validate one another in their respective roles as interrogator and interrogated. By restaging the different moments of the interview, the book confirms the existence of a prior agreement between the questioner and her respondent. In spite of the violence Guzmán hears about during what she calls her "long oral torture sessions with Romo," nothing obstructs the course of her dialogue with him, which continues on until the end of the interview without any further incident. No emotional outburst, no interruption of the controlled management of the exchange of questions and answers, no cracking of his voice, no knee-jerk response breaks the conversational fluidity of their unceasing dialogue. The sustained dialogic flow and Guzmán's unwavering tone lead us to believe that there was no disconnection that would undermine the pact of understanding assumed from the beginning (for communicative purposes) under the genre of "interview." Perhaps this dubious link of complicity between the two interlocutors, who fluidly take turns speaking to one another, is what the word "confession" was meant to disguise, substituting for the word "interview" on the cover so as to avoid any suspicion of implicit mediation/collaboration in the journalistic production of a truth induced and guided by the orchestrated rules of an agreement between the journalist and the ex-torturer.

The dialogic format of an interview presupposes not only a pact of recognition between interlocutors but also a certain communicative validation of the speakers' identities because the mechanism of dialogue situates the two individuals in a horizontal relation of "face-to-face" participation. Interviewing Romo meant validating him in a certain way as an interlocutor (even though some thought the interview was a trap designed to deceive Romo in order to obtain useful information), and this validation carried the risk of dignifying the undignifiable, of raising the inhuman to the level of the human, especially if nothing the interviewer says proves that this equal relation between the two speakers, assembled through the mechanism of an interview, was the result of any violence or explicit coercion. Throughout the book we even witness the revitalization of Romo's speech, which acquires more and more force as the book goes on ("Every one of his words makes his voice feel stronger, more powerful"[14]) without any sort of strong reaction from Guzmán that would demonstrate a vigorous attempt to reduce his threatening control over the conversation.[15]

When Guzmán does respond to Romo, she does it in such a discreet and measured tone ("Don't you think that, in spite of what you say – they were armed, they had military training, they wanted to overthrow the government – these people had a right to justice?"[16]) that we get the impression that, rhetorically speaking, we are observing a conversation about a disagreement between two perspectives which, although they are clearly opposed, both have the same basic right to be heard and defended. The restrained tone of Guzmán's responses to Romo gives rise to the idea that both interlocutors share the same repertoire of meanings (with regard to "human rights," for example) from which they can reasonably evaluate the divergences and antagonisms between their respective points of view. What the interview erases is the violence of the scandal that should have been evident in the verbal and ethical confrontation between one voice and another, the furious discordance of indignation: the abyss of incommensurability that should have separated the journalist's speech and the torturer's speech as two divergent ways of speaking that, formulated from the edges of morally opposed consciousnesses, have no recourse to any logic of sense in attempting to find some intermediary zone of argumentation and persuasion. There is no sign of any incommensurability

in the distance between questions and answers, no irrecon-
cilable rage that would attest to the moral and verbal abuse
committed by Romo – in the face of which Guzmán should
have been rigorously incapable of feigning tolerance.

It is curious that, when Guzmán takes up the theme of
"truth" ("You have to respond with the truth. To say what
you know clearly"[17]), that is, when she asks Romo to clarify
the dark reality of the practice of torture, she commits the
mistake of diverting the discussion of the term toward an
idiomatic question, ostensibly for the benefit of the broader
Latin American television audience: "You have to say what
you know clearly so that people who speak Spanish differently can understand you."[18] Guzmán reduces the problem
of "telling the truth" to a modulation of language that would
make Romo's repugnant account more broadly accessible to
all, without pronunciation errors, as if it were a matter of
comprehensibility that required this horrifying story, in spite
of its morally shocking content, to be made translatable into
a common language and to integrate itself into the communicative normality of everyday meaning.

The scene of torture

The interview begins with the neutral tone of a journalistic
investigator merely trying to confirm facts: "How was it that
you came to DINA?" ["¿Cómo fue que llegó a la DINA?"].
However, the conversation gradually accumulates so much
mutual confidence that at one point Guzmán says with
winking familiarity, "Hey, Romo ... Talk to me about your
conscience" ["Oye Romo ... Háblame de tu consciencia"].
The suppression of (professional) distance that is signaled
by the shift from the formal *usted* to the informal *tu* would
appear to be related to Romo's generally good disposition
toward Guzmán: "His aggressivity became an amicable
conversation that sought to keep me interested in what he
was saying"; "'You can use my radio to record, if you like,'
he offered"; "'You are patient, and you listen to what I say'";
"'In any case, you tell me if what I say is good or not.'"[19]

Even if the interview begins in a neutral, journalistic tone
that consists only of questions without commentary, pursuing

the objective recording of information, small subjectivizing mechanisms nonetheless take Guzmán into the (primarily grammatical) place to which Romo assigns her by convincing her that his story is addressed to her in a privileged way. To Romo's question "What do *you* want me to tell you?" ["¿Qué quieres que te *cuente?*"] she responds, "Why don't you tell *me* what happened when you were in the DINA?" ["¿Por qué no me *cuenta qué pasó con Ud. en la DINA?*"].[20] These two personal pronouns, in combined dialogue, dissolve into one another in a close-up that seems to exclude from view the audience, which is in the position of an omitted third term: the voyeur who intrusively listens to this semi-prohibited narrative.

Guzmán's journalistic motivation for interviewing Romo entailed crossing the threshold of the private into the public in order to bring out the torturer's hidden truth: from the introspectivity of the secret toward its journalistic dissemination. However, the game of pronouns in which a "you" and an "I" share the familiarity of an account of memory causes the private design of an *entre-nous* to predominate throughout the book. The enclosure of this *entre-nous* is first verbalized with the final chapter of the interview, which is shamelessly titled "The Evening Begins." The second affront consists of the failure to correct the oblique meaning of the chapter title "In Confidence," which was also the title given to the television program on which Guzmán's interview with Romo was broadcast. This reckless associative chain of words, which connote familiarity and intimacy (a chain of signifiers that the text is unable to decode), surrounds the interview with ambiguous and permissive signifiers that exult in roaming back and forth between the private and the public as if it were some kind of publishing achievement. The inappropriate way in which the text brings together the interviewer and the interviewee in an intimate setting with chapter titles like "The Evening Begins" and "In Confidence" validates someone who has done terrible things, and this critical carelessness subjects the reader to a true *abuse of confidence.*

In Chile, Guzmán's book is one more addition to an abundant collection of documentary, testimonial, and journalistic productions dealing with victims who denounced the violence with a language that was recovered (with no small amount of difficulty) from the physical and psychical disaster of torture. However, *Romo: confesiones de un torturador* does not collect any public (or already published) trace of Romo's victims' testimonies. It makes no explicit mention of this corpus of previous testimonies that demonstrate an expressive ability to narrate catastrophic identities. On the one hand, *Romo: confesiones de un torturador* tends to disregard writings by those who have already contributed their words to the conflictive sphere of social memory in Chile in order to fight for the victims' memory and dignity. On the other hand, the book propagandistically promotes the supposed truth-effect of the monstrous account offered by the individual responsible for the violence against them: "*And the most incredible thing is that these torments are recounted by the executioner himself.*" By saying that "this interview with Osvaldo Romo Mena is a document dedicated to the memory of a country,"[21] Guzmán seems to imbue Romo's story with the force of the truth of torture, which is demonstrably superior to the truth of his victims' powerless narratives. She thus allows the living memory of torture to be written in the torturer's memoiristic interpretation instead of basing her book's reconstruction of the past on the damaged narratives of his victims. However, the book does not only partially banish the public voice of the victims (who already gave their testimony) and bestow on the perpetrator's memories the task of supplementing the nation's lack of memory with regard to torture; it also gives Guzmán journalistic license to *represent* the victims in both the political and theatrical senses of the word: on the one hand, representing the victims through the delegation/substitution of their voice (she speaks in the name and place of "those who cannot narrate their own pain"[22]), and, on the other, adopting the figure of victim herself in a fictional montage which she offers to Romo.

We have already mentioned that the first agreement between the interviewer and the interviewee revolves around the value of language as a common currency between both. There is an analogy between journalistic interviews and police interrogations according to which both situations consist of "making speak," with the obvious difference that interrogation under torture subjects the body in which the secret is kept to methods of criminal violence. In both the interview and the interrogation, the point is to pull words out of the other's silence in order to turn them into useful information. The book unconsciously reinforces the analogy between journalistic interviews and police interrogations in the formal similarities that exist between the places where each of these situations occur: a cell that, both in the present of the interview (Santiago Penitentiary) and in Romo's past (the detention and torture centers), is characterized by the same "smell of incarceration, the urine and sweat of unwashed bodies." When Guzmán enters the cell to begin the first conversation with the ex-torturer, she notes: "Romo moved near a chair, asked to sit at the table with me, sat opposite me, and there we were, face to face."[23] This recreates the scene of Romo's pre-torture interrogations (without any self-reflection at all in the book on this poorly considered reference to the similarity of the two settings) through the resemblance of two scenarios of "making speak" that bring two subjects face to face (in both cases) inside a prison cell.

The interviewer gradually asserts her presence in the scene of the interview insofar as she first redirects the account toward her grammatical person ("Tell *me* how you used torture in the DINA") and later captures and directs Romo's attention during the television interview ("When we are doing the interview, don't look at the camera ... Look over here. *Look at me* ... because we are having a conversation").[24] Guzmán's sustained incorporation of herself into the scene of the interview with Romo culminates in an aberrant representation of herself in the position of the tortured body. This is perhaps the most abusive moment in the book, a moment in which Guzmán figuratively usurps the real place of the victim, offering her positionality to Romo in a degenerate vision that gives him the greatest pleasure: the image of a sexual victim.

Guzmán is both an individual and a character in a theater of memory that comes to life in the interview, playing with the realism-unreality of a hypothetical situation: "Let's say I have a sister named María. And my sister disappears. What should I do first to look for her body, to look for María?"[25] From this evocation of the role of someone looking for a family member who has been detained or disappeared, which she uses as a ploy to obtain information about real disappearances, the journalist places herself in the role of the torture victim to ask Romo directly, "*What would be the most efficient method for torturing me, for example?*"[26] This displacement of invented roles between the actual individual and a character gradually brings Guzmán dangerously closer to embodying the image of a victimized woman, which is to say, the image of the kind of victims that seduced Romo's imagination, which was particularly well known because his specialty was "the women prisoners brought to the torture centers, [who] suffered this sadist with his voluminous physique and his breathless panting. To the bodily horrors of torture, he added his perverted sexual obsessions."[27]

The book warns us in its first pages that, for Romo, "the cameras were exciting, as were the dark memories."[28] The book itself unfolds as the story of the preparations for a televised interview in which Romo will have to jog his memory in front of the cameras and recall the methods of torture he employed. The book tells us that, during the more than four hours of recording the interview, whenever Romo remembered something, "he smiled and rubbed his hands together," "his body gave off the ammonia-like odor of decomposing urine," and that "the interruptions in the interview were caused by the interviewee himself, who excused himself to go to the bathroom again and again." Romo's sadistic imagination, stimulated by the *camera* and the *memories*, finds in Guzmán's suggestion ("*What would be the most efficient method for torturing me, for example?*") a representation of the victim whose form serves to illustrate his perverse phantasmagoria. Confronted with the question (posed in the present of the interview), "How am I going to die?" Romo relives his past as the torturer who achieved sexual climax through a tension between body and word, the performative simulacrum of which physically recreates the past acts of torture and sexual abuse.[29]

The story of the interview ends when the "lights and sound" are turned off, and Romo utters one last obscenity: "There comes a moment when [the victim] cannot bear any more. There comes a moment when the person ... will do anything, they'll do anything. They'll tell you anything, they'll do anything."[30] These are the final lines of the interview which make the book explode in a vision of the torture victim's body being disassembled, while the torturer's story, overexcited by this bodily vacancy, achieves the sadistic and ecstatic climax of a verbality filled with visions of women's bodily remains.

We know that the tension between body and word dramatically occurs in the experience of torture itself and in its subjective re-elaboration. The mortifying force of the attack on the will in which torture pulverizes its victims is concerned primarily with destroying all connection between the abused body – turned into a pure suffering substance – and the expressive form of the word capable of articulating and uttering meanings. The post-traumatic elaboration of pain requires the victim to formulate images and representations that provide a frame of intelligibility for the remains of the broken body and spirit. It is recourse to the word (as occurs, for example, in the victims' voices in their testimonies) that makes it possible to transfer lived brutality to a level where experience becomes decipherable and reinterpretable through new constellations of meaning.

Thus, it is doubly worrisome that the book concludes with this destruction of the abject, feminine body of the torture victim, returning at the end of the interview to its primal dimension (of organic flows and excesses: urine, blood, excrement), while the torturer's story uses the word, occupying the victorious place of someone who *enjoys* the word, someone who can use and abuse words in the debauchery of a paroxysmal narrative. The memory of torture, mutely symbolized by the torture victim's inarticulate body, which comes apart in the chaos of indiscernibility ("they'll do anything"), is condemned by Romo's vicious eloquence to remain deprived of any ability to heal through speaking and naming.

To end the book with the image of de-structured feminine corporeality and the sexual explosion of its filthy substances is to punish once again the memory of the victims who still remember the extremity of the loss of one's being. This culmination of the interview, which is also the book's end, situates the victim's figurative representation on the edge of an abjection that excites the torturer's fantasies while stripping his real victims of any right to respond within the scenario established by the book. The torture victim's body is vacated ("they'll do anything") while the grateful torturer's satisfied account fills this void, consuming his sexual fantasy with the journalistic production of a false confession ("I'll tell you anything"). The sexual lapsus of this disastrous ending reveals the book's lack of vigilance in textually managing a horrifying account that should have carefully considered the weight of words and their narrative connections, because it is on these words (and on the practice of extreme caution in connecting them) that the crude exhibition of recollection depends so as not to violate the limits of the moral protection of the victims' memory.

Romo: confesiones de un torturador obliges us to ask ourselves if the specifics of horror, even though they serve to complete the truth of what has happened, should be fully revealed in their most prosaic details, knowing that overemphasizing horror tends to feed the voyeurism of the gaze. To refuse to yield to the sensationalism of doing away with memory is a way to stop the voraciousness of the market that devours horror live and direct and with consumerist delight. It is necessary to preserve certain aspects of the irrepresentability or unpresentablity of recollections that disturb the (available, exposed) image with which memories *nakedly* play, so that the remembrance of the horror does not lose its value as a refracting negativity amid so much journalistic sensationalism about the raw truth. It is a matter of categorically preventing the victims' dignified memory and the torturer's undignified story from ever being placed together "in confidence" in the same format.

5

Coming and Going

According to the National Security Doctrine of the 1973 military coup in Chile, "enemies of the Homeland" included anyone who resisted the totalitarian instrumentalization of order by a dictatorship whose primary ideological slogan was "to eradicate the Marxist cancer" and restore health to the population. Unidad Popular supporters suffered vengeful attacks against their bodies, ideas and ideals, structures of feeling, networks of symbols, and affects – anyone and anything that revealed a commitment to the revolutionary Left was targeted. Cut off from their country of origin for having been considered a potential threat that would "disturb the internal peace," thousands of Chileans were exiled from their homeland, finding refuge in various countries where they were obligated to reassemble the pieces of their lives, severed by exile and then put under the additional strain of the uncertainty of ever returning.

Active networks of international solidarity with the victims of the dictatorship united with human rights organizations, social movement organizations, and political parties to forge a vital outline of connection between the inside and the outside, as well as of the time before exile (the militant dream of a collective project of social transformation) and the unknown afterward (the longed-for return to Chile to continue fighting for the delayed triumph of a frustrated revolutionary dream). The testimonies of displaced Chileans narrate exile as a parenthesis of indefinite suspension between, on the one hand, a past sublimated by nostalgia for what was left behind and, on the other hand, the idealized future of an identity-based reencounter with the world that had inspired the Unidad Popular project.

The abundance of artistic and cultural productions created during exile was a response to the political urgency to muster international condemnation of the atrocities committed by the military regime. Determined by their circumstances, these artistic productions from exile compel support, basing their images and words on direct references to the political content of a message ("No to the dictatorship!") whose communicative efficacy was achieved by raising awareness among the audiences of international solidarity movements. Whenever these exiled creators returned to Chile, they modified the sphere of production and reception of the artistic and political message that had given strength and spirit to the culture of exile. This is when the true sadness of their uprootedness appears. No longer connected to the mobilizing forces of international solidarity that served as a remedy for the solitude of exile, they experienced an aggravated detachment from a country that had become generally unrecognizable to them upon their return, victims of an illusion cultivated over many years. "For some, exile lasted during the entire dictatorship and far beyond. Many returned before it ended ... Nevertheless, all suffered a traumatic return in which deception was almost always the dominant sentiment. The regime was ending, but it was clear that an arrangement had been made for its exit during the Transition. The country had changed too much. The aftertaste of the dictatorship was intolerable. And a staunch capitalism had been imposed, which exhausted and destroyed any hope of change."[1] After their nostalgia for the past of Unidad Popular (which had been preserved as a vital reference in the biography of exile), returning to Chile meant disillusionment and numbness for a social body that lacked sufficient energy to rebel against what could not have been anticipated from abroad: the civilian–military connection on which the institutional policies of the Chilean Transition were based, as well as national governance, which had been handed over to the economic domination of the neoliberal revolution.

The disconcerting present of reencountering the Chile of the Concertación alliance (which governed the country during the Transition years) frames the oscillation of memory in audiovisual works by Patricio Guzmán and Carmen Castillo, two Chileans exiled in Paris. Although they do so in different ways, the documentaries *La memoria obstinada* [Chile, Obstinate Memory] (1997) by Guzmán and *Calle Santa Fe* [Santa Fe Street] (2007) by Castillo are both characterized by the movement they endow to a memory that has been ruptured by exile, tracing a coming and going of fluctuating memory that relocates scenes and sequences as often as necessary so as not to be detained or trapped in the fixity of the cut.

Reconstructing the scene

Preparing for his return to Chile, Patricio Guzmán remarks in *La memoria obstinada*: "I have the memory of someone who has lived for many years outside his country. Someone whose memories have been embellished with the passing of time. *Will they now change when they come into contact with reality?*"[2] As a way of exploring the responses to this decisive question, which assumes the inevitable mythification of the past recorded in the exile's biography, Guzmán resolves to "bring to Chile copies of *La batalla de Chile* [The Battle of Chile] and to confront new audiences, some of whom will consist of the same figures featured in the documentary twenty years earlier ... in order to measure the transformations that not only time but also the experience of the dictatorship had brought about in these individuals."[3] *La batalla de Chile*, which Guzmán filmed in 1973, relates the final year of Salvador Allende's government up to the military coup of September 11 of that same year, which abruptly ended the production of the film. What stands out in *La batalla de Chile* is the camera's constant state of vigilance with regard to these extraordinary historical circumstances (which the filmmaker knows are unrepeatable) and its insatiable curiosity for capturing every moment and situation of historical reality in an increasingly dangerous situation.[4] The camera-witness of *La batalla de Chile* makes use of the truth-effect of reporting to record how the historical reality of Unidad Popular's revolutionary process is inhabited by a manifold verbality that, whether discursive or reprimanding, pervades parliamentary sessions, political meetings, neighborhood associations, union meetings, university protests, and conversations in the street. The militant, the didactic, and the assemblyist combine with one another such that, in the name of revolutionary consciousness, the alterations of the social/real that shake the Unidad Popular government's final year become the basis for permanent confrontations of perspective. The camera systematically prevents the central figure of comrade President Salvador Allende from displacing the secondary actors who enjoy the full freedom to invade the platform with their tireless oratory of the multitudes. Workers, housewives, and peasants share with political leaders, parliamentarians, and the comrade president the same, equal right to the free use of horizontally distributed speech. Nothing contrasts more with this wistful scene of yesteryear, filmed by Guzmán in 1973 for *La batalla de Chile*, than the passive scene of the Chilean Transition to which the filmmaker returns after his exile: a Chile whose formal democracy (neither participatory nor deliberative) excluded social movements from its decision-making processes; a Chile where the restricted use of public speech has been monopolized by the socioeconomic and communicative powers of official politics.

Guzmán's recovery and relocation of this historical citation of Unidad Popular and the bombing of La Moneda[5] is a means for restoring images that were prohibited in Chile during the Transition years – images from *La batalla de Chile* had never before been broadcast on Chilean television – and, moreover, to measure the impact of their cinematic reinsertion into a context of perception that had so notoriously changed. *La memoria obstinada* (1997) sets up an unsettling predicament between *knowing* (in the case of the filmmaker and the individuals featured in his documentary, having been direct subjects of the experience of Unidad Popular), *not knowing* (during the Transition years, Chile did not have the opportunity to reacquaint itself with the documentary archive of this filmic record of the final year of Allende's government), and *re-knowing* (actors and spectators meeting again with the drifting particles of a still-floating memory). *La memoria obstinada* restores the missing pieces of a memory that was interrupted twice: once by the overthrow of Unidad Popular and the bombardment of La Moneda, and again with Guzmán's exile, which prevented the people who appear in the film from ever being able to see the images he recorded. Aware of the potential missteps of returning to Chile, Guzmán fills the voids of disconnection (departure–exile–return), following the guiding thread of the memory of Unidad Popular, which he filmed with his own camera, thus adding what had been missing to the interval that was untraversed for almost twenty-five years due to the distance in both space and time between the filming of *La batalla de Chile* and of *La memoria obstinada*. Guzmán intersperses scenes from the past (in black and white) and the living present of today (in color) so that discrepancies in the memory of Unidad Popular might have the opportunity to generate ruptures in the normality of the everydayness of the Chilean Transition, which, interrupted by the event of memory, will react against this recollection.

The industriousness of the unsatisfied memory of an incomplete past, which returns again and again, never giving up, causes *La memoria obstinada* to reopen the archive of history (the coup and the military dictatorship), exposing it to present contrasts that generate variations and dissociations in the experience of memory. First, the documentary includes the commentary of several individuals who appeared in *La batalla de Chile* to return to these images in order to connect their present stories with their retrospective views on the past. Second, *La memoria obstinada* includes footage of Guzmán's 1997 exhibition of *La batalla de Chile* for new audiences who were seeing it for the first time (high school students, for example) in the hope that renewed counter-positions and views might help open up this film's vision of the past to interpretative debate. Both forms of rekindling the past generate intervals of non-coincidence between yesterday (memory) and today (remembering) that reactivate the accumulated layers of a troubled time in history.

More than remembering, *La memoria obstinada* (performatively) proposes *to make remember* by mobilizing a recollection that is both appropriate and dialogic in its modes of piecing together the experiences of the individuals in the film. Each one is asked to construct their own montages of memory, provoking associations and dissociations between the past and present, as they return to the same places that marked their lives more than twenty years earlier: a presidential guard returns to the Palacio de la Moneda; others go back to the Estadio Nacional [National Stadium] after having been imprisoned there, or they reunite with ex-members of Allende's Grupo de Amigos Personales [Group of Personal Friends] (GAP) to exchange information about what happened to their comrades, and so on. Certain biographical complexities that appear in these individuals' narratives in *La memoria obstinada* embed the figurative minutiae of the *intimate* in *La batalla de Chile*'s macro-historical frieze of the past, causing them to rub up against one another, but without the frictions that previous codes of militancy had generated, putting distance between them (the ideological-partisan on one side and the personal-subjective on the other). Guzmán produces a work of remembrance (to remember: to bring together scattered members) by connecting these fragments of disjunctive experience in a zone of personal encounters and significant liaisons. These private scenes in *La memoria obstinada* reduce the heroic-monumental tone of the past struggle and resistance of *La batalla de Chile* with the small, contingent stories of an I who tenuously narrates the singular-particular that individualizes every biography. Of all the individuals we reencounter in *La memoria obstinada*, only Ernesto Malebrán (who was also featured in *La batalla de Chile*) produces a rhetorical gesture of recollection that recapitulates the ideological mottos and the militant phraseology of revolutionary dogma, as if nothing had changed between *La batalla de Chile* and *La memoria obstinada*. Malebrán's tone clashes with the trembling minimality of memory that all the other individuals who appear in *La batalla de Chile* share under the same dubious register of "could be," of "perhaps": a register of the fallibility of judgment that, as a manifestation of the vulnerability of conscience, testifies to the state of defenselessness in which this historical catastrophe left its victims.

The connective and transitive character of remembrance in *La memoria obstinada* merges the searching and grasping of those subjectivities whom the rupture of the dictatorship and the obliteration of post-dictatorship memory deprived of the bond of "being-together." *La memoria obstinada* exercises this associative and collaborative force, carrying the "we" dispersed by the ruptures of history to new instruments of identification and recognition whose chain of transfer reveals the need of every memoiristic exercise to be supplemented and complemented by others in a collective labor of the coproduction of memory. This memory is redoubled in a memory-object (the recollection of September 11, 1973, captured in the photographs and archival images in *La batalla de Chile*) and a memory-subject (*La memoria obstinada*) which engage in dialogue through the movements the film assembles from among documentary photographs of the historical event and the personal reconstructions of each person's story.

In *La memoria obstinada*, these individuals fill in the gaps of one another's memories, and the sutured totality of these auxiliary versions reconstructs a delicate fabric of experiences of solidarity. The documentary's juxtaposition of these truncated versions helps to reconnect the broken threads of history, but it does so without trying to avoid the controversy of a historical recollection that admits of antagonistic interpretations, such as in the case of the students who passionately argue amongst themselves after having seen *La batalla de Chile* for the first time. The fact that the guiding convictions of *La batalla de Chile* are debated and re-debated in *La memoria obstinada* demonstrates to us how the gesture of liberating discordant passages in accounts of history and memory avoids abusing the orthodox narratives based on a faith in presumably undeniable truths about the past. There is a reason why the victims who speak up in order to remember constantly vacillate and oscillate: "I have my doubts," Carmen Vivanco (who has five relatives who were detained or disappeared) says when she is asked to recognize images and identify individuals. This hesitation and uncertainty constitute the chaste obverse of the victims who were made either to suffer the punishment of the authoritarian regime's triumphant speech and overbearing truths or to genuflect toward the intransigent dogma of revolutionary militancy. The individuals who appear in *La memoria obstinada* are bonded by the memories that biographically connect them in the act of recollection. No social exteriority explicitly links them to the national landscape of the Chilean Transition, which is perceptible only symbolically in Guzmán's documentary through a shot of Santiago that resembles a postcard picture. The view includes the Andes mountains (so often pined for by exiles as a geographical symbol of their return), which frames the hypermodernization of the city, the prefabricated image of which looks nothing like what Guzmán remembers. On arriving, the filmmaker stumbles across the Transition's decoratively ordered vision of this quiet land depicted in the postcard-picture vista. In *La memoria obstinada*, one of the individuals remarks that "we are like a cemetery, the final resting place of everyone we have been, everyone who has not died and who wakes up at the slightest everyday conjuring." Guzmán attempts to awaken what is in mortal slumber in the deepest recesses of memory by detonating a theatrical return of the past. This return of/to the past is provoked by a surprise performance of Unidad Popular's hymn, "Venceremos," by an orchestra in the middle of Paseo Ahumada: "For the first time in twenty-three years, in central Santiago the strains of 'Venceremos' resounded … Its author, Sergio Ortega, who lives in exile in Paris, has sent me the score, and a group of young musicians agreed to perform it, to the people's great surprise."[6] The performance orchestrated by Guzmán to put memory to the test of before and after "resulted in many young people looking on blankly, uncomprehendingly; some older men made brief gestures of surprise and disagreement and walked away hurriedly; another, quite serious man stopped and defiantly held up two fingers in the V-for-victory sign."[7] Guzmán's limit-experience of returning to his country consisted of submitting the Chile of the Transition – neutralized by the official placation of memory – to the effects of the decontextualization and recontextualization of a citation as symbolic as the hymn of Unidad Popular, blasted into the city's quotidian banality. This citation's defamiliarizing and alienating effect, which unfolds between filmed memory (*La batalla de Chile*) and the filming of memory (*La memoria obstinada*), measures how deeply the recollection of the dead has been buried and asks if it is even still possible to revive "a collective dream that has been smashed to pieces" (Guzmán).

The fissures of heroic memory

If the recorded images in *La batalla de Chile* that show Unidad Popular's process of social and political mobilization before the 1973 military coup is for Patricio Guzmán the origin scene that *La memoria obstinada* seeks to dismantle again and again, Carmen Castillo's *Calle Santa Fe* begins with the biographical memory of the two months when the filmmaker clandestinely lived in a house at Calle Santa Fe 728 with Miguel Enríquez, the top leader of the Movimiento de Izquierda Revolucionaria [Movement of the Revolutionary Left] (MIR), before the latter's death on October 5, 1974 and her subsequent exile. Her confessions about how "everything began in that house" or how "my memory always resurges from that house" make the event of Enríquez's death the recurring motif of a retrospective search that combines Castillo's personal history with the collective history of the MIR.

Castillo's coming and going through the memories that accompany her successive return trips to Chile, after several years of exile, repeatedly demonstrates an estrangement, a political and affective distance from her country, a country which had become hostile to her in the way that it symbolizes its "amnesia." The references she makes to her condition of exile consistently underscore her feelings of non-belonging: "To me, exile is the violent imposition of an abyss in the integrity of our references. *Nowhere, neither here nor there, do I read myself as complete. In every place, I am missing a piece of myself.*"[8] The question, "Who is returning to this country?," which *Calle Santa Fe* examines, reveals to us the search for an identity that has been broken by a rupture in continuity and belonging. Marked by this dissociative break, Castillo attempts to bring together separate pieces of experience: her life with Enríquez in the house on Calle Santa Fe; her activities during exile and her participation in international solidarity campaigns; her return trips to Chile and

meetings with her friends and family in which they discuss
the political decisions each of them made; the history of the
MIR, taken from archives that document the revolutionary
project of Unidad Popular; conversations with ex-militants
about repression and the underground movement. The
critical value of this memory reconstruction consists in the
fact that its author does not try to return to the originary
matrix of a unified self but rather strives to underscore the
mobility of the intersections that allow her to escape all fixed
identity: "[E]xile hardens your memories. Forgetting occurs
both when a memory becomes fixed and static and when it is
erased. *My fight is against a rigid memory that could become
stuck in place.*"⁹ Castillo's introspective and retrospective
exercise does not give in to the temptation either to fill in the
gaps of separation or to suture the cracks and fissures of what
remains incomplete. Moreover, the itinerant memory of *Calle
Santa Fe* avoids taking refuge in the certainties promoted
by the ethics of commitment that helped shape Castillo's
memories and instead freely investigates those zones of
doubt, ambiguity, and contradiction to which the rigidity of
stereotypical militancy paid no heed.

The dramatic expressivity of testimonies published in
Chile about the memory of the catastrophic dictatorship
is achieved through communicating the truth about the
criminal horror and terror of the Pinochet regime, the
evidence of which should provoke a universal, society-wide
condemnation. The ideological and partisan affinities of each
victim are bracketed because they might detract from this
condemnation, which should be broadly shared throughout
the entire community. There is no room for victims' testimonials to examine the positions of the Leftist revolutionary
struggle that articulates them through their shared militancy.
Castillo's *Calle Santa Fe* offers a testimonial that allows the
filmmaker, on the one hand, to address the model of political
subjectivity structured by revolutionary militancy and, on the
other, to learn about the aspirations and failures of the Left,
which is a result of the documentary's anti-dogmatic tone. The
self-affirmation of "*Nosotros los miristas*"¹⁰ (which functions
in *Calle Santa Fe* as a vector for bringing together archives,
documents, and testimonials about the history of the MIR)
would seem to be driven both by a need to communicate the

historical force and subversive vigor of this revolutionary project and by a personal obligation to know how to respond to the lacerating question that, starting with the historical defeat of the organization, runs as a subtext throughout the film: "*What is the meaning of so many deaths? Was it worth it?*" The search for arguments that respond to this question, which presumably few militants or ex-militants are willing to formulate themselves, is accompanied by the need to counterbalance reasons and circumstances for comprehending why certain so-called "revolutionary" actions within the political organization of the MIR itself were decided on by only a few (male) leaders in the name of everyone else. In contrast to doctrinaire accounts that repeat the myth and the legend of MIR heroes, Castillo dares to produce a documentary that leaves aside the heavy armature of the militant apparatus in order to immerse herself in the tumultuous interiority of the insubordinate construction of worlds.

At various points, Castillo's account shows signs of how taxing her life as a militant was, particularly with regard to the obligation to unbendingly fulfill a role tied to the morality of struggle and sacrifice that, such as the MIR conceived of it, should prevail at any price, even death. Read from the perspective of gender, Castillo's account shows us how the "feminine" as a symbolic configuration serves as a *fold* for introducing the dissonant and heterogeneous plural of the other (suspicion and rebellion) into the uniform principle of the One (dogmas and orthodoxy) and helps to crack the mold of absolute truths. Castillo remarks in the documentary that what felt most oppressive during her exile was "the repetition of the codes of the heroic widow." We may add to this comment her confessions published in a book dedicated to exile: "Survival ... An avenue, an apartment, they all look alike: suburbs of Rome, Stockholm, London, Ottawa. Wandering without vision, journey without movement, the same repetition of codes: the 'heroic widow' moves around blind, deaf, and almost mute ... From train stations to airports, I never stopped, one city to the next, meetings, press conferences, rallies. A full agenda. The character of the heroic widow was in demand. Obediently, I volunteered to play this role. My disgust grew."[11] The composition of the "heroic widow" is decomposed here as role, character, and

mask, demonstrating how these artifices of the configuration
of identity, designed to help maintain the structure of a
personality whose self is admittedly destructured, are unable
to provide a convincing foundation for a coherent identity.
Castillo's reflections in the book *Santiago-París: El vuelo de
la memoria* [Santiago-Paris: The flight of memory] (a number
of passages from which are interspersed throughout *Calle
Santa Fe*) offer us multiple signs about this non-fit between
person and character that reveal the contradictions of a
symbolization of nonconforming femininity, along with an
unconditional adherence to the roles programmed by partisan
militancy: "I know they can see my impostures ... Impossible,
the words escape me, I don't understand their meaning, I
stumble, stammering, confusing everything ... I learned some
phrases by memory ... My incompetence became obscene."[12]
Castillo's "somnambulistic" behavior during exile, which she
relates in *Calle Santa Fe*, shows her disaffiliation from the
preconceived role of the "heroic widow" of Miguel Enríquez,
a role which, outside Chile, she had to grandiosely embody
as a tribute to the memory of the MIR. Castillo's hesitations,
gaps, and lapses reveal the subjectivity of someone who has
experienced the oppressive role of living as an *example*, a
role she was obliged to embody by the morality of heroism.
The slogan "We the *miristas*" – that mark of enunciation that
gives shape to *Calle Santa Fe*'s introspective investigation –
recollects precursors of individual and collective memories
of the MIR without any obligatory reference to the revolutionary foundations that vertically (through men) conveyed
the heroic mandate. Rather, *Calle Santa Fe* highlights the
doubts and questions, the vacillations and oscillations that
would mortify the (masculine) political-doctrinaire cadres of
the historical MIR. The archives, interviews, and conversations that Castillo maintains with her ex-comrades in struggle
and resistance upon her return to Chile faithfully testify to
how militant dogma governed the revolutionary passion of
an entire generation intent on transforming the world. The
imperatives of militancy are spelled out: complete submission
and irrevocable commitment to the supreme cause; censure
for any attempted deviation from the triumphant teleology
of the sacred truth; the vertical orientation of organizations
called on to obey unquestionable orders; the moral rigor

of the order as sacrifice that can even include death as the maximum proof of militant loyalty and submission. Along with this faithful testimony, *Calle Santa Fe* presents Castillo as "already critical of the MIR culture of death" during the period of militancy that permitted no disagreement with the party framework or its founding principles. Her concerns about whether the decisions made by the political organization are clear enough – for example, with regard to "Operation Return," which, starting in the late 1970s, clandestinely reintegrated exiled MIR cadres, which meant that women were separated from their families for several years and forced to leave their children in Cuba under the care of the "Homes Project," organized by the Castro regime in solidarity with and in support of Chilean exiles. These concerns make visible some of the lines of contradiction that silently wracked women militants who faced the prospect of motherhood. Castillo broke through the barrier of unquestioning obedience to the validity of political decisions made by the male leadership of the MIR, creating space and modulation for negated affects and opening up a path to the intimacy of feelings for those whose personal sphere was censored by revolutionary slogans. *Calle Santa Fe*'s narrative, which is full of defiant impulses, demonstrates how the perspective of gender undermines the hierarchical alignment of the ideological party order that uniformly shaped militant behavior.[13]

The house on Calle Santa Fe is the referential core of Castillo's historical and affective memory, and her documentary reflects on the MIR in the context of the Chilean Transition that appears to be unmoved by the exalted memory of the past of the militant Left. One of the desires that guides Castillo's final trips to Chile for filming the documentary is that of wanting "to reappropriate the house ... to give life to the memory of the fallen." This reappropriation of the place marked by Enríquez's tragic death defends the memory of the militant Left from being forgotten, and it transmits the political energy of an earlier desire to historically transform society. Nevertheless, in her conversations with new militants and leaders still connected to the historical MIR, these latter express in Castillo's documentary their "weariness" with efforts "to maintain living memory through homages."

According to them, the ritualization of making a heroic figure like Miguel Enríquez into a symbol of resistance, rather than revitalizing the memory of the MIR's insurgent past, might truncate inspiration for present revolutionaries and prevent new social forces from seeking out their own forms of action, allowing themselves instead to be mimetically influenced by the repetitive codification of the past. Present political leaders cause Castillo to see that the conversion of Enríquez's house into a "memory site" expressly dedicated to homage would be a reification of memory. In the documentary, Castillo understands that memory has no reason to remain stoically loyal to the past in order to be truthful, and that it should instead be receptive to the transformations of the present so as to be able to account for the insubordination of one's own words – that it should be assumed as an insubordinate memory. Castillo thus rejects her initial objective and decides only to "mark" the house. "Marking" the house means recording that this site, Calle Santa Fe 728, was occupied by Miguel Enríquez before his death and that it contains a memorable past, and furthermore that a will to inscribe signs should gather together the traces of that valiant past so that it does not disappear into oblivion. However, at the same time, the marks of this memory of a place cannot remain confined to reductive commemoration, which would isolate Enríquez's memory from those territories of collective existence that disseminate the recollection of the MIR both singularly and heterogeneously. By deliberately breaking with the script of a merely restorative memory of the legendary past, *Calle Santa Fe* gives a critical sense to the bifurcation between *memory in itself* and the altering transfiguration of a *memory for others* that is based on traveling and located in zones of passage.

6

Architectures, Stagings, and Narratives of the Past

The spaces of memory constructed in post-dictatorial societies – national monuments, memorials, museums, and other spaces, generally under the pressure of demands for truth and justice by human rights movements – serve to make more publicly visible the material traces of the repressive past and to cause these traces to remain active in the formation of a citizen consciousness that continues to interpellate society with the ethical imperative of "Never again!" Every space of memory produces its own strategies of commemoration and remembrance to pay public homage to the victims and to give an expressive and communicative value to the condemnation of the violent past, resorting to different aesthetic, symbolic, political, and institutional maneuvers for staging this memory. Reviewing the scenic compositions of these manipulations of language, form, and signification helps us to decipher the kinds of memory practice proposed by these commemorative spaces. For example, they help us to distinguish between those efforts oriented toward simply transmitting the emotive dimension of a memory of comfort and sorrow and those that aim to demarcate a critical position and intend to influence the social and political uses of memory.

Villa Grimaldi

The group of witnesses and survivors of Villa Grimaldi, formerly known as the "Terranova Barracks," where more than 4,500 prisoners were incarcerated during the military dictatorship, saved the Villa from a double erasure: the disappearance of the place where bodies had disappeared as a result of a concerted effort that twice attempted to bury the site and conceal the evidence of the dictatorship's crimes. Under the modernizing subterfuge of urban renewal, the discourse of progress – in complicity with the economic and commercial interests of real estate developers who profit from the very soil of the city within the neoliberal regime – sought to liquidate the accounts of the memory of violence contained in those former detention and torture facilities. What better way to demonstrate that the ethical drama of human rights violations had become incompatible with the celebration of consumption in the market society of the Transition? Preventing the grounds of Villa Grimaldi (located in the Peñalolén district of Santiago) from being swept up in the current of investment, urban planning, and real estate speculation was an urgent and necessary response to efforts to crush the vestiges of the reprehensible memory represented by the Terranova Barracks under the weight of construction machinery. The establishment of Villa Grimaldi Park was at least able to protect one layer of the commemorative traces of tragic memory connected to the land by preventing it from being triumphantly purchased and thereby devastated. This would have only contributed to an acceleration of the ludicrous economies of profit. However, what map of memory is traced out by the stones and gardens of Villa Grimaldi, which has now been converted into a memorial park?

The visitor walks through a park that stages memory on the surface of the land, in an open area that seems beyond horizons when compared to the dimension of closure and darkness of memory marking the repressive past of imprisonment and torture. How can a space so free of walls be capable of recreating the asphyxia of incarceration, the confinement of the cell and the blindfold over one's eyes, the condemnation of darkness and the imprisonment of the senses? What relation can be established between, on the one hand, the gaps of the mind perforated by fear in the dark past of prison cells and, on the other, the levelling of this system of lines and regular proportions that gives the present-day visitor the relaxing clarity of a spatial openness that was entirely unavailable to the prisoners, submerged as they were in isolation and confused by impediments to their vision?

The flat geometry of Villa Grimaldi Park today relies on the prominence of the gaze in order to see from its heights the reminders of violence traced on the ground. However, the eye and the gaze are apparatuses for physically distancing oneself from the object that, by exercising and coordinating control over perspective, turn everything they see from above into distance and abstraction. The homogeneous spatiality and geometry of Villa Grimaldi Park turn what was a shattered *texture of experience* into an ordered *field of vision*. The prominence of perspective disembodies the living material of memory whose deep subjective fractures are unrecognizable in this serene, featureless space, leveled out as if it were designed for quiet strolls and picnics. And what can be said about the recycled, Pompeii-style mosaics that adorn the placards and fountains of Villa Grimaldi as a reference to the original tiled surfaces of the bathrooms where torture was inflicted? This citation is so ornamental that it ends up situating the lacerating memory of torture in a banal landscape that renders all recollection completely anodyne.

Many of the testimonies written by victims of the dictatorship refer to the hell that Villa Grimaldi once was. These testimonies, extending from the source of the torture (an apparatus dedicated to pulverizing the connection between body and speech), must narrate the unnarratable of a limit experience: passing through the threshold of destruction to extract words that are capable of modulating the break in speech caused by the mortifications of identity they endured. The shaken voices of the survivors of Villa Grimaldi testify to the torture they suffered, and they oppose to the abolition of reason and meaning the resurgent power of *naming* (once again connecting words) so that their horror can become meaningful and transmissible. The testimonies written by the survivors of Villa Grimaldi pierce us with the tremendous echo of voices broken by torture that emerge from the limit between the disarticulation of the body and the rearticulation of the voice. The tormented echo of these surviving voices becomes completely inaudible in the quiet landscape of the Villa Grimaldi Park for Peace. All that is left are the names of places marked by ceramic plaques: "Torture chambers, electrified metal beds, torture rack"; "The Tower: site of solitary confinement, torture, and execution." These place markers are characterized by a naive didacticism that presumes that such a literal identification of places and objects in the calm silence of the park gardens could actually reveal something of the terror suffered by the victims inside the now absent buildings. The writing of these words ("solitary confinement, torture, and execution"), composed and arranged with ceramic pieces in a harmonious mix of different colors, names the darkness of the hell of Villa Grimaldi, but it does so in a design modality completely foreign to the dissolution of the referential and semantic universe experienced by those who were viciously reduced to the inarticulation of meaning by methodical procedures that aimed to eradicate their consciousness. It is the same with the Rose Garden at Villa Grimaldi Park, where each rose bush bears the name of a disappeared person on a terra cotta medallion: the redemptive quote "We were all going to be queens" written on the fountain surrounded by flowers connects poetry (Gabriela Mistral) with a conventional poetic motif (roses). The floral poeticization of the environs of Villa Grimaldi Park, converted into an idyllic landscape thanks to this Rose Garden, causes the disembodied memory of the sexual violations against women imprisoned there to evaporate. Is it fair to allow this idealization of femininity (the rose as a symbol of love and beauty) to erase the imperative to remember how the women imprisoned at Villa Grimaldi were treated like kidnapping victims and subjected to a masculine domination that unleashed sexual violence against them, particularly when we consider that their status as political militants betrayed precisely the kind of idealization of womanhood associated with gender stereotypes, such as, for example, the romanticism of flowers?

In the second stage of the renovation of the Villa Grimaldi Park for Peace, two scale models were added in a belated

attempt to provide a material anchor for the physical memory
of the torture facilities, reconstructing "the Tower" and "the
Cell" that were used to incarcerate and torture prisoners.
One must ask whether the compulsory installation of these
scale models into the natural landscape of the Park, stripped
of any historical or documentary contextualization, subverts
in any way the overly peaceful image of the memory of
Villa Grimaldi. This image of memory, by ornamentally
cultivating the embellishment of the prison ruins, removes
the rawness of the facts associated with these scale models,
which have been architectonically integrated into the meticulously landscaped environment. Villa Grimaldi Park was
conceived of as a site for paying respect to the dead and as a
park for reencountering life at the beginning of a democratic
transition that was not willing to tolerate any eruption of
memory that might disturb the consensus-based discourse
of reconciliation.[1] The Villa Grimaldi project emphasizes
the coexistence of people and groups (the park as a meeting
place for reunion and unity), which even acquires a religious
sense – death and resurrection – in the cross that is formed
by intersecting paths in the Park, converging at a baptismal
fountain that lends a Christian inspiration to the harmonious
rebirth of a community in peace: a community called on to

Image 1: Villa Grimaldi, Rose Garden. Photo by Alejandro Hoppe.

follow a path that during the Transition served to displace citizen grievances from the juridical and institutional sphere of punishment to the symbolic and moral dimension of forgiveness. Villa Grimaldi Park adorns the ruins of memory with the pacified convergence of severely diminished spirits – a contrast to the cruelty of that which remains unfinished in matters of truth and justice: a cruel incompleteness that must not be softened by the melancholia of ruins so beautifully converted into a comforting landscape.

The Cementerio General de Santiago: memorial of the disappeared

Cemeteries are places for burying the dead and for circumscribing death – that is, for delimiting the scene of the funeral ritual and separating it from the sphere of the living. Designating a cemetery as the fixed residence of the disappeareds' phantasmal missing corpses is an attempt to alleviate the pain and uncertainty of their disappearance, which condemns them to eternally wander like unlocatable specters. Establishing a place for them in a cemetery allows their unverifiable death, the non-place of their disappearance, to finally find refuge in the mortuary convention of a culturally assigned resting place.

The large white wall of the Memorial for Missing Detainees and Persons Executed for Political Reasons in the Cementerio General de Santiago is engraved with the names of 3,079 victims of the dictatorship. On both sides of the Memorial are empty burial vaults waiting to be filled by the bodies of the disappeared who are yet to be located or identified. What stands out is that the predetermined number of these empty vaults does not coincide with the total number of the disappeared indicated as still unidentified on the Memorial plaque. It is as if the arbitrarily determined number of burial vaults were speaking to us about the symbolic need to put an end – with a number – to the interminable and incomprehensible lists, as if confronting the fear of losing count of the damage caused would in some way contribute to this simulacrum of certainty. The non-equivalence between the fixed quantity of spaces reserved for bodies and the number of names of the disappeared listed on the Memorial is evidence of the unsettling doubt that anxiously surrounds the undefinable answer to the question "*How many are missing?*" Without establishing an *exact* correspondence between the number of bodies and the number of tombs, the arbitrariness of the number of vaults reserved for missing remains figuratively condemns the *lack of all measure* between loss and restitution, between truth and justice. The paradox of the incongruity between the number of vaults and the number of names on the list of the Memorial of the Disappeared reminds us that the damage caused by forced disappearance is not quantifiable from an economy of calculation because there will never be any true proportionality between the loss of the loved one, the remains of disappearance that only allow us to remember them in part(s), and the rations of justice that are intended to partially repair the absolute damage.

In front of the plaque at the Memorial for Missing Detainees and Persons Executed for Political Reasons, four faces are carved in stone and turned skyward with their eyes closed in a gesture of remembrance and piety, seeking to symbolize humanity (the essence of the human). These faces are accompanied by a quote from the poet Raúl Zurita, which reads: "All my love is here and has remained here fixed to the rocks, the sea, and the mountains." The stone and the rhetoric of the public memorial consolidate and eternalize memory. The four faces carved in stone in front of the memorial wall are an attempt to universalize the features of suffering; however, this universalization petrifies the human being in the sublimity of a transcendent humanity. The archetype of the human face memorialized in stone kills the physiognomic singularity that, in contrast, pulsates in the photographs of the disappeared, which their families rescued as traces of beings who are unique, which is to say, irreplaceable in their individuality as recognizable people. The metaphysics of suffering, which transcendentalizes the carved stone of the four faces turned upward toward eternity in the Cementerio General, negates the nontransferable particularity of the features of the missing detainees' faces in their photographs, whether from ID cards or family albums. Facing the machines of disfiguration put into motion by the dictatorship, the photographic images of the disappeared combat the serialization of non-identity which condemned them to the status of "unidentified" by reestablishing the physiognomic details of each victim's identifying features. By abstracting and essentializing, by transcendentalizing, the stone of the memorial is indifferent to the *singular-biographical* element of the photographs that give the disappeared the contours of their individuality. This individuality has been snatched away from the victims – not only because of their disappearance but also due to the genericity of the very category "disappeared" – through the suppression and omission of their particularities. The atemporality of the stone, which transcends the contingence of humanity, kills the latency of the *not yet* (past–past) and of the *still* (past–present) that causes the technique of photography to waver ambiguously in the tension between the absent and the present, the real and the unreal, the tangible and the intangible. The sculptural memoriality of these solemn, carved figures in the Cementerio General ossifies remembrance and offers a petrified version of the memory of the victims, whose pious faces, absorbed in the infinity of the divine, appear to be disengaged from the contingent battles of political and social memory that continue to be fought around this site with every commemoration of September 11, 1973.

On one side of the Cementerio General is Patio 29 where, starting on September 11, 1973, bodies of victims of the dictatorship were clandestinely and anonymously buried. With the return of democracy and the public revelation of a number of criminal acts that had been hidden as military secrets, investigations of Patio 29 in 1991 resulted in the identification of the remains of 107 people on the list of the disappeared. The discovery of the remains of previously unidentified individuals and the restitution of the bodies to their families made it possible for these latter to progress through the work of mourning in order to assimilate their loss symbolically once material evidence of it was produced. However, in 2006, it emerged that the Medical Legal Service reports that had identified the victims' remains contained errors, and that these errors communicated to the Concertación Ministry of Justice, where they were met with silence based in either neglect or political expediency.[2] The victims' families thus had to confront a double loss (first, of their loved ones' bodies, and second, of the certainty that the remains that were discovered were actually theirs) and a double deception (the frustrated expectation for a body that never appears and then the appearance of remains that were mistakenly attributed to the disappeared). The administration of Michelle Bachelet formed a Presidential Commission that resolved to turn Patio 29 into a "memory heritage site." A plaque marks the place where the bodies of the disappeared were buried with the following text: "After it was discovered that the remains of 48 people were mistakenly identified, the State of Chile issued Exceptional Decree 91 on July 10, 2006, declaring Patio 29 as a national historical monument. Today, Patio 29 has become a site of collective memory, of the practice of remembrance for the families who saw their lives cut short by mistaken identity but especially by society in general." The reappearance of the remains after the disappearance of the bodies executed by the dictatorship and the news of their mistaken identification during the democratic transition put into motion a disastrous sequence of burials and exhumations of identities, the covering up of truth, and the discovery of error. This disastrous sequence undermined any possibility for the families of the victims of

Image 2: The Cementerio General de Santiago. Photo by Alejandro Hoppe.

Patio 29 to rest assured in the truth of a confirmed death. In fact, the work of mourning precisely entails that "to know is to know *who* and *where*, to know whose body it really is and what place it occupies – for it must stay in its place. In a safe place."[3] From the non-(re)cognition of the military regime's victims to the false assignation of names that mistakenly identified the bodies during the transition, the history of Patio 29 shows us that, no matter how much a plaque on a public monument insists that its efforts to honor the victims have a reparative value, the non-conclusion of the encounter between disappearance and reappearance undoes any pretension toward definitive closure – regardless of whether or not it was ordered by institutional decree. The injury caused by identity as absence and failure persists: *"They were unidentified. They had names, and once again they no longer exist."*[4]

The Bulnes Bridge

The Bulnes Bridge is a site that has been marked multiple times by both military violence and its commemoration. Various plaques memorialize Father Joan Alsina, a worker priest executed there in 1973, as well as the murders of seven employees of the San Juan de Dios Hospital, five Catholic priests, and fourteen residents of the Puente Alto neighborhood, which all occurred on this bridge at different times and in different circumstances. The various commemorative plaques on one side of the Bulnes Bridge (which crosses the Mapocho River, where bodies were often dumped during the dictatorship) face a mural with the painted quote, "Face me when you kill me, I want to see you so that I can forgive you," which were Alsina's final words to his executioner. This is the place chosen by photographers Claudio Pérez and Rodrigo Gómez to build a Memory Wall composed of the portraits of 936 missing or killed detainees printed on ceramic tiles.

Also located at the Bulnes Bridge, which is already filled with public memorials, Pérez and Gómez's Memory Wall combines photographic rhetoric with previous tributes to memory, including sculpture (Claudio Di Girolamo) and muralism (the Camilo Torres United Muralists). By locating their marks of remembrance in an area where there are a number of memorials to victims of the dictatorship with differing artistic formulations and varying levels of technical expertise, Pérez and Gómez's photographic mural invites the citizen's gaze to become an implicit part of critical reflection on how memory is symbolically modulated in terms of composition and representation, which is to say, in terms of the operations of signs and formal techniques that place the cultural value of memory within a particular expressive register.

By choosing this bridge for the site of their memorial, the creators of the Memory Wall make a gesture inverse to the one that pays tribute to the disappeared interred in the Cementerio General. Instead of commemorating the victims in a corner demarcated and separated from the quotidian world of the living, the Memory Wall was placed near the high-traffic zone of a bridge where multiple urban transit routes intersect. The wall does not attempt to concentrate memory in a sacred place (the cemetery) that induces withdrawal and self-exclusion from the traffic of the city, but, on the contrary, it tries to deindividualize the act of remembering and make the memory of the disappeared intersect with the everyday routines of the living community that populates the fabric of the city. No longer limited by the conventional rituality of the cemetery, the memory of victims of the past is scattered throughout Santiago, randomly blending with the itineraries of anonymous passersby.

The drama of disappearance has remained ciphered in the black-and-white portraits of the disappeared that their family members carry in front of themselves or on signs at human rights marches. The technical apparatus of the photographic image always speaks to an absence of the body (subtraction) through an effect-of-presence (restitution) that temporarily pulsates under the divided register of the living dead. The portraits of the disappeared are testimonies of identity that respond to the desire to remember the victims in the particularity of their biographical and existential details, which were erased both by the machinery of torture and disappearance (the suppression of the person and the de-identification of their condition as a person) and by the administrative dryness of the language of the Human Rights Commissions that archived their information in a mass of numeric files.

Many of the portraits engraved in the stones of the wall at the Bulnes Bridge show the disappeared in everyday poses from photo albums: pictures in which they are calmly confident that their lives would continue, even though they were suddenly cut short by military violence, with nothing in the defenseless pose of the portrait predicting this future homicidal interruption. The photographs of the victims trace the innocence of a "before" that knew nothing of evil, and now they are replete with auratic pulsations generated by the way they sustain that unrepeatable moment in which the disappeared believed that they would always be safe. The abyss between, on the one hand, the unconcerned face of the disappeared who still knows nothing of the imminent tragedy and, on the other, the present day from which we heartbreakingly see the photo of this person who was made into a victim of history composes an unexpected *punctum* (Barthes) that moves and deeply affects the gaze that openly views them today.

The portraits of the victims were printed on ceramic tiles and embedded in the mural at Bulnes Bridge. How can one not read in this choice of material a symbolic tension between memory and forgetting? Due to its characteristics, ceramic speaks to us of the impermanence of prints, marks, and erasures through the relation between adherence and impermeability that defines this material. The tiles show the tension between the recording of an inscription (memory) and the aseptic enamel of the tile, which, designed to be mark-proof, ensures that the residues of preexisting materials can be cleaned off the surface. By using tiles to record the commemorative traces of photographic remembrance, the Memory Wall works with the contradiction between *inscription* and *de-inscription*. Pérez and Gómez try to influence the way in which the present dissolves the opacity of the detritus of the past (human rights violations) as a reminder of a threatening, obscured, infectious time contaminated by historical filth (ideological conflicts and antagonisms), a time that wanted to obviate the Transition in the name of democratic governability.

The composition of the photographic mural at the Bulnes Bridge includes numerous spaces with missing tiles that

Image 3: Bulnes Bridge. Photo by Alejandro Hoppe.

correspond to the portraits of 256 people who were disappeared and never found. The missing portraits publicly testify to the incompletion of the memory of their disappearance. Unlike monuments that, with a rhetoric of heaviness and solidity, try to stabilize historical memory with a definitive meaning, the mural at the Bulnes Bridge posits that memory is knotted together from the precariousness and incompleteness of a process of remembering that remains open to interruption, fragmentation, and erasure. The missing portraits point to the non-completion of waiting as a condition of the reflexivity and deciphering of an unfinished memory. Pérez and Gómez's Memory Wall functions as a "counter monument" (James Young) that, from the unfinished, the pending, and the deferred, provokes questions (in full public view) about the relationship that continues to exist between the gaps of disappearance and the fissures of memory.

Londres 38

Between September 1973 and December 1974, the building at Calle Londres 38 in central Santiago functioned as a

Dirección de Inteligencia Nacional [National Intelligence Directorate] (DINA) detention facility where eighty-three men and thirteen women (two of whom were pregnant) – most of them younger than 25 years old – were executed or disappeared. Perhaps one of the main characteristics of this memory site is its location right in the middle of Santiago, near government offices, courthouses, the stock exchange, and the ex-headquarters of the military junta. How could these executions have been carried out so secretly that no material trace of the crimes could be found? How was it possible to live so close to this evil, maintaining an urban banality that never took notice of the horrors taking place in the streets and neighborhoods of central Santiago? It is as if the location of this place of torture and death were a warning sign of the everyday indifference of the multitude that refuses to see the evidence of atrocities or distracts itself from the memory of them with the distractions of entertainment.

The plan to mark this place as a memory site was never intended to immortalize its memory. The proposal submitted by the architects of Colectivo Londres 38 (Macarena Silva, Fernando Rojas, Heike Hopfner, and Pablo Moraga) intended to play with the language of the pedestrian path by placing a sign on the pavement in front of the house at Calle Londres 38, along with 280 tiles of white marble and black granite embedded in the cobblestones, discreetly evoking the tile floors of the building that prisoners were able to see through their blindfolds. This reminder of the tile floors subtly acts as a generative matrix of memory by alluding to the reports, repeated many times in different testimonies, that "through the tape over my eyes I could see the black and white tiles." Displaced from inside the house (the private) out into the street (the public), this remembrance set in tiles calls on passersby to revisit the same act of the Londres 38 detainees, whose blindfolds allowed only for furtive, downward glances. Despite knowing that pedestrians in the city are attracted by the bright lights of consumption and thus look upward or to the sides, these memorial tiles on the pavement act as marks of the painful past that cause the gaze to stumble. In addition to these tiles are ninety-six iron plaques arranged on the pavement listing the names, ages, and political affiliations of the victims murdered there, the majority of whom were connected to the Movimiento de Izquierda Revolucionaria [Movement of the Revolutionary Left] (MIR). The work of the recovery of Londres 38 thus demonstrates the exceptionality of its political memory as one of the few projects in Chile in which party affiliation is considered relevant to the recreation of the historical record of the disappeared. In contrast to the general tendency to subsume information about political affiliation under the universalizing category of the passive, innocent victim, Londres 38 affirms "the right to know and critically evaluate the memory of militancy and the history of the political organizations that at different points in our history, particularly in the 1960s and 1970s, sought to transform society and to make it more just, equal, and participatory, and then in the 1970s and 1980s resisted by any means within their capacity the imposition of the terrorist regime of the state."[5]

The house at Londres 38 was renumbered "Londres 40" by the military dictatorship to thereby render nonexistent the crime scene that could serve as material evidence confirming the allegations of human rights violations committed there. One of the first gestures of critical appropriation of this memory site consisted of reinstating the original house number – Londres 38 – thereby erasing the gesture of erasure that had perversely desired to substitute one address for another as yet another strategy of deception, simulation, and concealment of evidence. Colectivo Londres 38 was founded in 2008 and resolved first to reject the Chilean state's (bureaucratic) request to transform the site into a planned Institute for Human Rights and then to refuse to comply with the museistic conventions of the "memory site" genre, which tends to appropriate memory into the language of art collections.[6] In a gesture of double insubordination, Colectivo Londres 38 told the state that perhaps the recuperated house would serve better as a point of encounter to maintain open – or in process – a collective reflection on the complex meanings of the *mise-en-scène* of memory during the shift from dictatorship to post-dictatorship. This may be why Londres 38 has been considered "the only place that can break the intransitive memory of Chilean commemorative monumentalization and its permanent enclosure in the world of the victims."[7] By intertwining the too easily posed question of "what to do with the place" – as if memory should confine itself to the same physical space where past events occurred – with the other (interrelational, dialogic) question of "what can be done from this space," Londres 38 attempts to avoid anchoring memory to its original location and instead activates multiple connections with other vital energy sources.[8]

Conversations between heterogeneous groups of people (surviving victims, relatives of the disappeared, academics, artists, and thinkers) were held at Londres 38 as part of the process of collective self-reflection on the fate of the site, which took place in a house that was overflowing with memories but completely empty. At these meetings, some members of the group expressed the desire "to make the place speak" through documentary, theatrical, or pedagogical-communicational interventions that would perceptually try to recreate the horrors of the past based on survivors' testimonies. This alternative – "making the place speak" – seemed to hold that only the realism of a documentation loyal to the dramatic quality of lived experience would be able to inspire in visitors an awareness of the senses and thereby lend an irrefutable presence to the knowledge of the true past. Another alternative debated at these same meetings suggested that, instead of "making the place speak," silence should be imposed on the vacant house as the only gesture radical enough to communicate the emptying out of representation generated by the horrifying events that took place there. Up to the present day, Londres 38 has resisted the figurative dramatization of memory and the mistrust of the "sanitized past" with which various memory sites attempt to make the horror of torture more accessible, more examinable. Londres 38 relies instead on the shock felt by visitors who know the history of the place, the labyrinth of this empty house, which physically aligns the bareness of its walls with the sensation of helplessness due to the absence of any indication of what the victims experienced as prisoners there. If it were to provide signs about the memory of the place to communicate its past via didactic instruments for educating visitors about the horror, the house at Calle Londres 38 would certainly become inhabited by the uninhabitable quality of a space burdened by psychological and physical abuse. Perhaps what

Image 4: Londres 38. From the Londres 38: Espacio de memoria Archive, 2009.

is intolerable – uninhabitable – in the memory of torture occurs through the inhospitality of remembering a vacant space that cannot orient itself through the reconditioning efforts of museistic practices. Ensuring that these critical questions about approaching the problematic nexus between violence and the staging of memory are kept open, Londres 38 continues to work – always in a plural way – on the dilemmas of representation, such as the very problematic knot of the treatment of memory.

The Museum of Memory and Human Rights

The Museum of Memory and Human Rights building in Santiago rises up above an esplanade that leads to the main entrance, where engravings of the thirty articles of the Universal Declaration of Human Rights solemnly greet arriving visitors. It is as if the Museum wished to dispel any apprehensions on the part of a (Chilean) society that fears confronting its past, establishing the Declaration of Human

Rights as a frame of legitimacy that, by clothing itself in a seemingly unquestionable validity based on its "universal" condition, confers authority on the Museum's activities, which were subject to dispute from the very beginning. The display of the Universal Declaration of Human Rights serves to justify the Museum's public mission to anyone suspicious about the timing of this institutionalization of the victims' memory, when the divisive potential of past conflict continues to exist.

The exterior of the Museum of Memory has been clad with copper plaques, a material that serves as a clear reference to Chileanness as a value of national identity with the aim of reinforcing the bonds of an integrated "we" in response to the risk of community division over the meanings of a disputed past. The interior of the Museum is notable for the luminosity provided by windows, a light that seemingly desires to eradicate the shadows and obscurities of that dark history and instead privileges the transparency of open surfaces that dispel any sense of enclosure.[9] Because the Museum of Memory architectonically constructs its narratives of memory on the basis of a formal apparatus, it is useful to examine the choice of transparent glass, which materializes the desire to uncover long-hidden memories of the repressive past in order to make them publicly visible finally, exposing to the light of day all the damning evidence that had been hidden through censorship. The translucence of the glass windows – bringing to light, making it easier to see, exposing to the light of day – metaphorically indicates to us that the politics of dissimulation that covered up the military regime's homicidal violence has ended, and that the construction of the Museum of Memory and Human Rights is the institutional ratification of efforts during the Transition to make this suddenly available memory into a memory-exhibit. However, the architectonic construction of the Museum works with ambiguous materials and meanings owing to the fact that its exterior, which is clad entirely in copper, presents an impenetrable building that prevents anyone from guessing what transparencies exist inside. This ambiguity between transparency (within) and impenetrability (outside) unconsciously reflects the sociopolitical tension between the available and the reserved, the unarchived and that which has a restricted circulation, like that still-latent tension that runs throughout a society in which many secrets of the past are still kept out of the reach of ordinary citizens.

The Museum of Memory and Human Rights, like many other memory sites, relies on the testimoniality of scenes and objects that make memory tangible. There are also the archives and documents that, beyond the senses, provoke readings of the historicity of the events in which collective experience is inscribed so that memory will not be exhausted in the emotionality of private recollection. We could say that the Museum of Memory and Human Rights, along with its exhibition of a few real objects that physically testify to the suffering of the victims of torture and incarceration, has a tendency to surround these objects with photographic images, audiovisual material, testimonies, and archives that act as information sources for the visitor to use to acquire a greater knowledge of the facts and to form judgments about the history and memory of the period. The Museum of Memory and Human Rights endeavors to complement the realistic real of the objects (for example, the torture rack called "*la parrilla*" ["the grill"]) with survivors' testimonies, which articulate perceptions and develop interpretations of their own memories, thus helping to break the silence of those who suffered with images and accounts that can manage mobile trajectories of subjective reconstruction and collective identification.

The way in which the Museum of Memory and Human Rights combines strategies of presentation and re-presentation of what happened, alternating exhibited materials (objects and victims' testimonies) with expressive apparatuses (such as audiovisual technology), might be considered adequate insofar as it elevates what is *mediated* in the work of memory, which has been called forth to reconfigure the past. Unfortunately, however, the Museum of Memory is dominated by a museography that weakens the intensity of the memories of the violent past by theatrically establishing a decorative aesthetic that removes any weight, rigor, or seriousness. One example: photos of the disappeared are included as part of a montage installation that places them in a high, almost unreachable place on a wall separated from viewers by glass windows that delimit and frame the space

Image 5: Museum of Memory and Human Rights. Photo by Cristóbal Palma. Archive: Museum of Memory and Human Rights.

of recognition. This space is adorned with plastic candles with a hyperstylized design that completely fails to reflect the drama of the evanescence of memory. The excessive distance interposed by the glass in this architectural montage places the victims' portraits in a situation of distance and spectacle that nullifies the melancholic trembling of the aura: "It is no coincidence that glass is such a hard, smooth material to which nothing can be fixed. A cold and sober material into the bargain. Objects made of glass have no 'aura.' Glass is, in general, the enemy of secrets. It is also the enemy of possession."[10] The artificiality of the candles and the excess of transparent distance that affectively de-links the photographs of the disappeared from the gaze of the viewer constitute a flamboyant and failed demonstration of this theatricalization of montage that makes the design seem cultish, industrialized by the market of styles with which the Museum of Memory all too seductively plays.[11]

7

Two Stagings of the
Memory of YES and NO

October 5 continues to be an important date in Chile as it marks the day of the national plebiscite in 1988, which consisted of a vote for the options of either YES or NO. This plebiscite brought an end to Augusto Pinochet's control of state power after more than fifteen years of dictatorship. In spite of the dilemma the Left faced in having to accept rules established by a political and constitutional panel that the dictatorship itself designed to serve its own interests, the plebiscite became a wager – a bet at the polls – that the military regime could be defeated, thereby opening up paths of convergence between the democratic desires available at the time.[1] The choice between YES (to continue the model imposed by the dictatorship, which garnered 44.01 percent of the vote) and NO (for a democratic reopening under the form of a transition government, which won with 55.99 percent of the vote) polarized Chilean society with a divisive power that was expressed with particular emphasis in the television ads that each side was allowed to broadcast every day for fifteen minutes during the month prior to the election on October 5, 1988. This was the first time since the beginning of the dictatorship in 1973 that any opposition to the military regime was given access to television audiences. By choosing audiovisual language as the ideological and discursive basis of the political campaigns' advertising efforts, the 1988 plebiscite confirmed the latest role of mass media in a newly neoliberal society, one in which the military government promised to donate a television set to every Chilean household to ensure that the entire populace would be able to receive the military junta's official propaganda – as well as advertisements designed to encourage consumerism and to promote the market society model the dictatorship had implemented to domesticate collective subjectivity.

The memory of the 1988 plebiscite forms part of diverse constructions of social memory and politics concerned with how to resolve the transition from dictatorship to democracy in Chile. While some readings tend to highlight the fact that the audiovisual basis of the plebiscite campaign advertisements and their televisual effects were a determining factor in the NO vote's ultimate triumph, others emphasize the historical precedent set by the construction of a citizen-based opposition to the dictatorship – without whose efforts the result of the plebiscite would never have come to pass, regardless of the NO campaign's successful televisual tactics. This perspective later protested that in the NO campaign's televisual promotions the more combative images of this collective struggle were displaced by more anodyne images.

It is interesting to reflect here on the relationship between images of the past (already recorded memory) and the displacement of its traces (the transformative reinscription of the past in a future–present) by analyzing two representations of memory: the first is aesthetic (Pablo Larraín's 2012 film *No*[2]), and the second is social and political (the imaginary of the YES/NO dynamic which resurfaced in the last Matthei–Bachelet presidential campaign in September 2013). Both stagings of memory allow us to consider how the same historical memory – the 1988 plebiscite – can play either a *dehistoricizing* role, as in the case of Larraín's *No*, or a *rehistoricizing* role, as in the case of the 2013 presidential campaign, which, at the same time as the fortieth anniversary of the coup, caused this memory to be recharged with the power of the present in a moment when the country found itself at a new political crossroads.

The mimesis of memory

Larraín's film – which was lauded at its world premiere at Cannes in May 2012, where it received the Art Cinema Award before becoming the first Chilean film selected for the Academy Awards in Hollywood – tells the story of the 1988 Chilean plebiscite through the portrayal of the conceptualization and production of the NO television campaign. Larraín's film recreates the circumstances in which the television campaign producers opted for "a happy, playful, poetic tone influenced by advertising,"[3] which was intended to prevent their efforts from being perceived as a threat to anyone who might not be immediately sympathetic. The NO campaign's call to vote, "Without fear, without hate, without violence," entailed opening up a path toward reconciliation for a divided society that, after a broad democratic convergence began to express an interest in the recuperation of democracy, had to learn how to peacefully organize the transition and leave aside the rancor of the bitter past. Larraín's film shows the way in which advertising was integrated into the NO television campaign, using numerous video clips to highlight the luminosity of happiness (let us recall that the slogan of the movement to recover democracy was "Happiness is coming") and thus to dispel social and cultural prejudices against an allegedly grim and resentful Left.

Some critics with Leftist political inclinations decried the lack of substance in the film's plot, which they claim diminished the 1988 plebiscite's historical transcendence by emphasizing instead the NO campaign's creative televisual work, which was directed by media and advertising experts. These critics claim that Larraín's film ignores the social forces of popular protest that, in and through the plebiscite, opened up a breach in the dictatorship and brought about Chile's passage toward democracy. Therefore, they allege, the film exaggerates the television campaign's role in the democratic recovery. Effectively, these critics claim, *No* omits the collective struggles of the Chilean people and privileges the referent of *advertising* in the history of the plebiscite electoral campaigns. First, the film's plot and characters focus on the advertising world, from where the producers of the NO television spots were recruited. The campaign was made up primarily of Leftists who found themselves in the position of relying on advertising agencies to surreptitiously produce the NO campaigns television ads while also trying to survive professionally and economically during the dictatorship. Second, the film emphasizes advertising as an acceptable guise for the image as commodity-form in the era of cultural hypercapitalism, using a mass language that seduces the imaginaries of modernized society through media technology. Third, *No* reveals the advertising model to be a new form of political communication that allows technical expertise and electoral marketing to displace and replace ideological commitments. Finally, Larraín's film attempts to demonstrate that advertising was merely the outermost layer of "democracy as a product," and that the 1988 plebiscite was formulated in the context of the transition to a market society that had already given itself over to the pragmatism of transactions between power and money.

Some Chilean critics have read *No*'s aestheticizing maneuvers and cosmetic image as evidence of a *parodic strategy*. They claim the film relies on the simulacrum of advertising in order to connote the weakening of historical meaning in a nontranscendent world where the macro-narrative of politics has evaporated in the face of individual (anti-political) micro-fantasies of private consumption.[4] Read as a satirical work, *No* is thus a denunciation of the constitutive ambiguities of the Transition, which has had to forge a way between the forced inheritance of the dictatorial past and the self-limiting promises of re-democratization. In this way, Larraín's film parodies the "disguised" Chile of the Transition years: a Chile that, as Tomás Moulian argues, had to don "democratic garments" in order to hide its economic and institutional dependence on structures inherited from the dictatorship.[5] *No* helps us to understand how the NO campaign anticipated the Chile of the Concertación administrations, which had to sacrifice the *base* (history and ideology, the politicization of citizens) in order to take advantage of the *forms* (the market as a substitute for social relations).[6] However, what happens when critique or parody moves casually between denunciation and celebration?

Satire and parody are postmodern devices characterized by ironic citation that typically mock dogmatic ideas about representation as an originary and transcendent notion of truth through the use of duplicates and replicas that ambiguously constitute the border between the signifier and the signified, the model and the copy, reality and fiction. Undoubtedly, Larraín's cinematographic aesthetic is inscribed in this game of parodic and satirical fictionalization, and it ridicules any pretense of unmasking the "real" truth of history and society, opting instead to cover the referent (history) with the masks of artifice and simulation. Yet, we can ask of Larraín's *No* the same question Hal Foster posed with regard to a certain postmodernist aesthetic: "[W]hen does montage recode, let alone redeem, the splintering of the commodity-sign, and when does it exacerbate it? When does appropriation double the mythical sign *critically*, and when does it replicate it, even reinforce it *cynically*?"[7] The answer to these questions presupposes the ability to verify whether art – cinema in this case – can open up an emancipatory potential that makes it possible to break with the uncritical separation between the "activity" and the "passivity" of the gaze: a passivity of the gaze that becomes obedient to the spectator in the way they receive the work's predetermined message instead of transforming it into a co-participatory critical elaboration of meaning. In Larraín's *No*, memory is unable to retrieve what is lacking from an uneasy past: "a form of consciousness, an intensity of feeling, an energy for action."[8]

One of the principal artifices in *No* is the way the film plays with the indeterminacy of experiences of *déjà vu* as false recognition of the past in the present, and vice versa. Larraín's film attempts to recreate the atmosphere of the era by using the same U-matic video technology that was widely used at the end of the 1980s (when the television ads for the plebiscite campaigns were recorded) in order to give the images filmed in the present the appearance of images from the past.[9] *This blending of time periods* is a semiotic device that functions in the film as an *operator of anachrony* insofar as it freezes memory as the past–past. *No* causes the *present of recording* to blend its images together with *the recorded past* by filming a movie in 2012 with equipment and technology from 1988. This blurring of time periods causes the present of filming (time-in-production) to regress toward the past of the filmed (archived time), preventing the sociopolitical changes that took place in the interval that separates the original (the 1988 plebiscite) from the copy (Larraín's film about the plebiscite) from being incorporated into the viewer's memory-production.

What are the new expectations of a society that, between 1988 and 2012, emerged as a *present in process* capable of modifying the relationship between the politics, market, and democracy installed by the advertising-based version of the plebiscite Larraín claims he wants to criticize? Without a doubt, these expectations came out of the student movement of 2011, which advocated an escape from the market-based consciousness that had captured Chilean society in the trap of "democracy as a product," which Larraín's film ironizes.

It is true that the audiovisual wager of the NO campaign in the run-up to the 1988 plebiscite vote prefigured the triumph of advertising, design, and marketing that would become dominant languages in Chile and which, along with the economy and mass communications, dissolved the substance and weight of ideology in the superficial light of media technology. It is useful to recall that the book *Los silencios de la revolución* [The Silences of the Revolution] (1988) by Eugenio Tironi, one of the main conceptual authors of the NO campaign, explained that Chileans headed to the polls to vote in the plebiscite were "not rejecting the modernizing project of the dictatorship," and that the NO option "did not propose any end to the [neoliberal] economic model (rather, they were careful not to do so)."[10] Even though the discourse constructed by Tironi and the ideologues/advertisers of the NO campaign lamented the social costs of the "structural adjustment" of neoliberalism's "shock therapy," they did not offer any refutation of the modernizing developmentalism of a macro-economy committed to growth.[11] Nor did Tironi reject the hegemony of the market which, in its diversity, placates the tastes of all consumers, thus generating the illusion of a "'multiple choice society."[12] But if the dominant aspect of this economic and cultural logic of the market society continued to operate in the same mode during the long years of the Transition, this logic was emphatically interrupted by the 2011 student movement.

In interviews related to the promotion of the film, Larraín insists that he was trying to criticize the model of the democratic transition that was prefigured by the NO campaign's advertising strategy. When the film premiered in Chile, the director's staff publicized certain meetings with leaders of the student movement, who had taken to the streets shouting the slogan "End profit!"[13] However, the aesthetic Larraín uses in his cinematic construction of the memory of the 1988 plebiscite and the significant effect it has on the film contradicts his stated intentions of sharing the student movement's critique of neoliberalism. By blending today with yesterday through the artificialization of an indefinite past–present, *No* preserves the memory of the 1988 plebiscite in a fixed image that contradicts the dynamic of coming and going required of a memory in action. The artificial simulation of a filmic statement that erases the *production of the present* in favor of the *reproduction of the past* causes the film to deny historicity in three ways: as passage, as interference, and as becoming. The cinematic overlapping of the past and the present in the mimeticism of a falsely recognized and unaltered yesterday prevents *No* from being able to *update* the past and *reorient it toward the future* by displacing the contexts of yesterday and today.

The antagonisms of meaning and the conflicts of value surrounding the past of the dictatorship and the transition are disputed by the interpretative systems of political and social memory. Larraín claims that in his film he attempted to formulate the following question: "Is the plebiscite merely the defeat of Pinochet, or is it also the victory of Pinochet's model?"[14] In order for this (decisive) question to be present in the film and activate a potential critical movement around the meaning of the democratic transition inaugurated by the plebiscite, it is imperative to refrain from confusing the *recorded traces* (past) with the *filming of its replica* (the present *as* past). As Paolo Virno argues in relation to the effect of *déjà vu*:

> The state of mind correlated to déjà vu is that typical of those set on *watching themselves live*. This means apathy, fatalism and indifference to a future that seems prescribed even down to the last detail. Since the present is dressed in the clothes of an

irrevocable past, these people must renounce any influence on how the present plays out. It is impossible to change something that has taken on the appearances of memory. As such, they give up on action. Or, better, they become *spectators* of their own actions, almost as if they were part of an already-known and unalterable script. They are dumbfounded spectators, sometimes ironic and often inclined to cynicism ... To [their] eyes, the historical scansion of events is suspended or paralysed; the distinction between "before" and "after," cause and effect, seems futile and even derisory.[15]

By revising the past as a recorded copy of the present that functions as an imitation, *No* erases the intervals of dissatisfaction and nonconformity that separate the already-was (the 1988 plebiscite) from the not-yet (the aspirations for a different future expressed by the 2011 student movement, which critically reread the history of the Transition and appealed to its unconsumed virtuality). Larraín is correct to say that the plebiscite was established as "the victory of Pinochet's model" – a restricted democracy besieged by neoliberalism – but it only existed in this way in the imaginary of the Chilean citizenry until the civic-military desire for perpetual order was vehemently contested by the 2011 student movement, which was able to subvert the narrative of the forced agreements between two foundational postulates: the social economy of the market and the depoliticization of the citizens.

The fetishization of advertising (the metaphor of "democracy as product") on display in *No* stifles the critical work of deciphering those traces that silently contradict their original inscription in the hope of some kind of disquietude that would provide the power to conjoin them transformatively in an open sequence of past–present–future.[16] The over-aestheticization of the replica generated by Larraín's film discourages this disquietude of conscience, causing the 1988 plebiscite to become socially inactive through a flirtation with post-history (the neoliberal consensus that disregards any antiestablishment or utopian impulse) and post-politics (in which there would no longer be any contrast between different societal projects because they will have blurred the lines of ideological antagonism).[17] Fortunately, sooner or later memory presents itself in such a way that the desires for change that were opposed in the past (those popular desires obstructed or delayed by the aesthetics of the political marketing of "democracy as a product," which dominated the NO television campaign) can have a second chance to be expressed in a future–present of history attuned to the revelation that it is never too late to restore a different past in the present: a past modified by the *deferred* realization of its unkept promises.

Theater of antagonisms

The commemoration of the fortieth anniversary of the military coup in September 2013 coincided with the most intensive phase of the presidential race between two women, both daughters of dictatorship-era generals: Evelyn Matthei and Michelle Bachelet, whose fathers were on opposite sides during the 1973 coup.

Matthei, daughter of ex-member of the military junta Enrique Matthei, was one of the most well-known and recognizable figures of the feverish television campaign aired in support of the YES option in October 1988. The recorded memory of Matthei expressing her support for Pinochet in these television spots, along with the simultaneous commemoration in 2013 of both the coup (September 11, 1973) and the plebiscite (October 5, 1988), transformed her into the public reincarnation of what had become an almost unmentionable position even on the Right, after Sebastián Piñera, the president at the time, had called voting for the YES option "a mistake."[18] With this shameful memory attached to her 2013 presidential campaign, Matthei was marked by a line of continuity that fatally linked her historical support for the military dictatorship to her candidacy: a candidacy that was manifestly opposed to the changes expressly desired by the majority of the population – reforms covering taxes, labor, education, and the Chilean constitution. An additional reinforcement of this connection is the fact that Matthei's campaign manager was Joaquín Lavín, who during the dictatorship wrote the book *Chile: revolución silenciosa* [Chile: Silent Revolution] (1987), which expounded triumphantly on the modernizing changes that were taking place under

Pinochet's dictatorship, changes synthesized by "the growth of the workforce, the creation of systems for pensions, higher education, and health; the number of televisions per household, and exports."[19] From that point on, the program of the Alianza por Chile [Alliance for Chile] party (led by Matthei) continued to reaffirm a society that prioritized the defense of individual freedoms over social rights, promoted private enterprise and free competition of opportunities as incentives for entrepreneurship linked to private property and the logic of consumption and investment, considered personal well-being to be based on increased consumerism, and encouraged competition as a never-ending calculus of the advantages and disadvantages of individuals reduced to winners or losers. Nothing about Matthei's earlier positions seemed to have changed much since her support for the YES option in the 1988 plebiscite (favoring the neoliberal experiment promoted by Chicago School economists that was so convincingly defended by Lavín in *Chile: revolución silenciosa*) and the present of that electoral year of 2013, when Jovino Novoa (historical leader of the UDI[20] and Matthei's main defender and protector) insisted – forty years after the fact – on affirming that "profit or gain is the very heart of the social economy of the market ... for without profit, there is no incentive, and without incentive there is no progress."[21] The Lavín–Matthei–Novoa axis served as the backdrop of the Alianza slate and reinforced a continuous sequence between the past (1988) and the present (2013) of the Chilean Right, linked to the legacy of Pinochet: a sequence that very eloquently demonstrated that the Right continued to show the same desire to expropriate the public and the community for the benefit of private interests, which had been securely protected by the authoritarian State Constitution of Jaime Guzmán in 1980. The image of Matthei espousing YES campaign propaganda in 1988, which was recorded and then rebroadcast by the media, projected onto her 2013 presidential campaign the indelible image of her support for Pinochet, thus intensifying the image of a YES/NO (Matthei/Bachelet) dynamic that restored the power of negativity to historical memory, precisely at the same time as the commemoration of the military coup.[22]

From within the sphere of political theory, Chantal Mouffe argues that the radicalization of democracy presupposes "political passions" that are mobilized around divisive borders separating clearly distinguishable social projects.[23] The anti-political (neutral, impartial, de-ideologized, economistic, technocratizing) vision of a world supposedly located "beyond the Left and the Right" is a falsely disinterested vision that, by postulating "that political questions are ... mere technical issues to be solved by experts," is actually aligned with the Right.[24] At the other extreme of this depoliticizing vision is the "Leftist" recovery of the contentious dimension of the social and the political – a dimension that, with its identifications of *for* and *against*, revitalizes the demarcations of positions in hegemonic debates about the meaning of the social, which the technical and instrumental neutrality of neoliberal consensus tries to hide. It is not that "Left" and "Right" name fixed, overdetermined identities bound once and for all to a homogeneous and closed-off "being" or "belonging" through a univocal definition. Instead, "Left" and "Right" designate locations on the map of mobile, contingent, and relational cultural ideologies. The primary division between "Right" and "Left" (understood as borrowed names or tactical identifications) can be traced from the border that separates those who, on one side, admit that there is no social construction without antagonisms of power or hegemonic disputes, and those who, on the other, seek to neutralize historical conflicts under the de-ideologizing figure of post-politics as a simple technical instrument of social administration and planning. This distinction between *politicization* and *depoliticization* was applied to historical memory in September and October 2013 as a result of the game of antagonisms reignited by the controversial specter of the 1988 plebiscite that loomed over the presidential race between Bachelet and Matthei.

For the UDI campaign, led by the same Evelyn Matthei who supported the YES vote in the 1988 plebiscite, the historical past is a limitation from which we must be liberated. First, because the memory of the military regime has over time become politically inconvenient, even for the Right. Second, because the neoliberal Right nurtures the presentism of a society in thrall to the calculus of feasibility of merely operational logics (of the flat and straight time of management); a presentism that negates the historicity of social practices as representative trajectories and collective projects. The neoliberal Right, with its expediency of order, does not recognize that the framework of the traces between past, present, and future is a bond of social and historical construction of identities and communities that is rearranged as past–present–future every time different modalities of the possible reappear – whether in the re-reading of the *already-happened* or in the invention of the *to-be-done*. In contrast, the NO of the "No to the Right" proposes the valorization of the historicity of the social, which is to say, the vital possibility of collectively experimenting with history in the narrative of each event. During the Transition years, the pragmatism of the Concertación administrations annulled the troubled dimension of the social by subjecting voices and behaviors to a rationality of consensus (the "democracy of agreements") that reduced the intensity of ideological conflicts between divergent visions of history and society. The student protests of 2011 marked an enthusiastic rupture with the *anti-ideological neutralization of politics* that had been imposed by the Transition government, establishing their slogan of "End profit!" as a challenge to the right-wing thesis so ardently defended by Lavín, Novoa, and Matthei. What the 1988 plebiscite had anticipated as a transition to "democracy as a product," mimetically re-envisioned by Larraín's film, was virtually obliterated by the force of confrontation with memory (the memory of the YES and NO campaigns of the 1988 plebiscite at the same time as both the commemoration of the fortieth anniversary of the military coup and a highly polarized presidential campaign), which, by combining itself with a future designed to be open to the heterogeneity of the social, reactivated the weakened energies of the past and endowed the memory of the plebiscite with a new political character.

8
Past–Present: Symbolic Displacements of the Figure of the Victim

In order for the memory of the past (of the dictatorship and its victims) to be endowed with the power of interpellation in the present, we need an account of the past that leaves open the networks of signification for a memory and which must remain unfinished so that it can renew its powers of public invocation and convocation out of the breaks and fractures in the narrative that call forth new critical assemblages.

This is evident with regard to the "Londres 38 Memory Space": neither the memorial (the material and symbolic architectures that honor the victims) nor the documentary (the historical evidence; the tribunals' reports that situate the criminality of the acts in objective terms) suffices to bring forth memory into the present and disseminate its traces beyond what is circumscribed by the victims' suffering. Neither the documentary nor the memorial is enough to keep alive – in action and movement – the memory of human rights violations. It is therefore necessary to bring together this memory of the past *into the present* in order to achieve a transformative reactivation of remembrance that might enable it to undertake new intersubjective explorations throughout society.

In 2011, the Londres 38 Memory Space commemorated the International Day of the Disappeared through a collective urban intervention consisting of ten artists' work, which were placed in different locations throughout the Alameda in Santiago, the main boulevard of which divides the city.[1] The choice to locate the intervention along the Alameda was the first sign that the intervention would favor a mobility of memory between the past, the present, and the future.[2] This is because the echoes of Salvador Allende's final speech at La Moneda still resound with their promise that someday "the great avenues [*las grandes alamedas*] will open again where free men will walk to build a better society." Every time the Alameda is occupied as the site of citizen revolt, the resonances of that memorable phrase make it possible to envision the future (figuratively) and pass through the catastrophe of the dictatorship (the 1973 military coup) with the call of a utopian becoming that continues to speak (in deferral) to the new forces of social change. When the past of a tragic memory is perceived as incomplete (not finite), it virtually remains on the course of realization as a suspended time: a time in reserve with latencies and potentialities that will be expressed in the future thanks to a memorial labor of recording and unrecording of the traces that disrupt historical duration so as to open up within itself spaces for difference, fissures of noncoincidence between the *completed past* and the *past being completed* that expose this contingent and transitive memory to the hazardous multiplicity of new intersections with an unknown present.

On the International Day of the Disappeared in 2011, the Londres 38 Collective invited ten artists to interpret the tragic meaning of the forced disappearance of persons. However, Londres 38's invitation was not an attempt to repeat the well-known past (the parade of photos of the victims of the military dictatorship) but rather to invite meditations on the alterations of an unknown or unrecognizable present: the present of the disappearance of Mapuche youth José Huenante, who was arrested by Chilean police in September 2005 and whose whereabouts remain unknown up to the present day. His case has been considered the first case of "forcible disappearance" in democratic Chile. It was, as the Londres 38 Collective described it, the gesture of "uncovering the case of José Huenante, a Mapuche 16-year-old who disappeared in September 2005 after being detained by police":

It occurred in a democracy. At the time of Huenante's arrest and disappearance after being taken away in a patrol car, President Ricardo Lagos was the occupant of La Moneda, and the investigation (which found nothing that resulted in any kind of justice) has been continued under the governments of Michelle Bachelet and Sebastián Piñera. The case, currently under the jurisdiction of the Military Justice department, remains unsolved. The forcible disappearance of persons, which was a systematic practice during the years of state terrorism imposed by the civilian-military dictatorship, is in this case a shadow from the past that looms over the present.... Therefore, the idea was proposed to 'visibilize' Huenante and thus, along with him, to bring into the present all those who disappeared in earlier decades.[3]

Some of the artists who participated in the urban intervention chose to incorporate into their works Huenante's identification card photograph. One of the primary iconographic rituals of memory for the victims of human rights violations under the dictatorship has involved ID card photographs carried by family members or displayed on signs during demonstrations and marches. These ID card photos, as fading black-and-white copies, encapsulate the melancholic aura of incomplete mourning. Huenante's more recent ID card photo is in color, and, in addition to his youth, this underscores (along with the shift from analog to digital) the modernizing advance of the identification procedures of civil registration. The first temporal disruption of past memory (the black-and-white photograph) of the commemorative ceremony in honor of the disappeared was also a disruption of past ceremonies, the visual impact of which had an alienating, defamiliarizing effect on the signifier "portrait" with the use of a color photograph. A reminiscence of the past (the International Day of the Disappeared) and a transfiguration of memory: a conversion to the electronic language of the identity card of someone who disappeared in the present.

Huenante's photograph, reproduced multiple times and enlarged on ten artworks placed along the Alameda, adds a new type of victim to a historical sequence that includes the routine confiscation of identity cards during the dictatorship. This is produced by the visual impact of a modernized portrait, introducing a contemporaneity to the gaze that views the drama of disappearance, warding off the danger of the anachronistic temptation to render the photograph in black and white. Huenante's image generates instead a technological mismatch – between the black-and-white photocopies and the color photograph – disturbing the gaze that observes the past. That is to say, it produces an out-of-jointness that removes the past from the passive conditioning of ironic repetition and then acts as a source for the reinvigoration of the perceptual material of memory.

The visual grammar of identification card photographs is evidence of the police apparatus of capture and seizure of identity due to the fact that it is the medium through which disciplinary societies keep track of their subjects in the interests of obedience and control. New systems of identification and civil registration defend modernizing technology (and its digital code), arguing for the need to guarantee citizens' security and prevent the damaging effects of identity theft. Huenante's color ID photo, displayed on the same scale as the city itself, lays bare the ironic and cruel deceptions of the regulating discourse of "public safety" as a form of security supposedly able to prevent crimes against individuals. Worse than having his identity supplanted, Huenante's personhood was wiped from the face of the earth. The artistic, large-scale photographs of Huenante's identification card photo situated along the Alameda betray the state of insecurity to which the discourse of "public safety" abandons marginal subjects (in this case a young, poor, Mapuche) who are anonymously subtracted from public circulation and disappeared in a blur of civic invisibility. Situated in the center of the city, Huenante's portrait becomes the bearer of a renewed charge against the erasure of identity. Along with continuing to denounce past military repression during the International Day of the Disappeared ceremonies, the case of José Huenante reveals the present news of the state's indifference and the incompleteness of justice in response to new cases of disappeared persons who, in an intensely neoliberal landscape, occupy the most disintegrated borders of the map of social integration. Huenante's photograph therefore remodels the symbol of disappearance, breaking with the repetition of the emblematic black-and-white figures of the dictatorship's victims. Yesterday (the terrorism of the state) intersects with today (the Mapuche conflict), causing

different victims to converge in a diverse signifying vector
(the helpless, the defenseless, the mistreated, the ignored, the
devalued, etc.) that points out new criminal aberrations of
public safety laws.

On the reverse of Huenante's identification card, the
following information is printed: "Place of origin: Mapuche
Nation." This (stigmatizing) mark predestined him as a
victim of ethnic discrimination due to his status as a member
of an indigenous community in Chile, dispossessed of his
political rights. In their statement, the Londres 38 Collective
chose to relocate the characterization of this victim from one
repertoire to another: from the persecution of ideological
opponents of the military regime (yesterday) to the violations
of identity committed in a neoliberal present (today) that
humiliates and slaughters subjects who are considered super-
fluous because they are not useful to the capitalist production
of surplus value. Some persecuted subjects are *in excess* and
therefore can be treated by the market society as *less valuable*
subjects because they do not factor into the accounting of
profits. By forcing everyone's gaze onto Huenante's subal-
ternity (for which he was oppressed), the urban intervention
coordinated by the Londres 38 Collective repoliticized the
memory of forcible disappearance, causing the convergence
of two different methods and temporalities for instilling fear:
the state terrorism of the dictatorship (yesterday) and the
threat of anti-terrorism laws (today) that continue to crimi-
nalize the origin and status of the indigenous Mapuche.

Luis Correa Bluas, the Huenante family's attorney,[4] has
asked, "When did José Huenante disappear? Early on the
morning of September 3, 2005, taken into custody by police
agents of the Chilean state. When did he stop being visible
to this same state? Probably the moment he was born."[5]
Huenante's identification card was digitized in order to
certify his identity. However, after a person disappears, the
only remaining trace of their identity is this card, which now
refers to a John/Jane Doe, an unidentified person: someone
stripped of all features and distinguishing marks. Huenante
moved from "invisibility" to "disappearance" without ever
benefiting during his precarious life from the state network
of public guarantees that might have helped him as a subject
endowed with rights. The Londres 38 intervention exposed

the city to the fact that Huenante was so invisible that his disappearance itself passed by unnoticed, even after the "dictatorial darkness" had been replaced by a (supposed) "democratic transparency."

The Alameda is a site of maximum spectacularization due to the boulevard's saturation by advertising billboards. The photographic contrast between, on the one hand, the seductive visibility of bodies offered by consumer advertising and, on the other, the opacity of José Huenante's negated existence superimposed on enlarged photographs dramatizes the comparison between bodies of pleasure and bodies of rejection and condemnation. The Londres 38 intervention brought an identity devalued by the state to be evaluatively framed in portraits that urged citizens to contemplate the appearance and disappearance of subjects on the basis of the following question, formulated by Judith Butler: "Whose lives are regarded as lives worth saving and defending, and whose are not? ... whose lives are considered valuable, whose lives are mourned, and whose lives are considered ungrievable?"[6] José Huenante's life was never a life "worth saving and defending" or worth being "mourned" by the state's public security apparatus. Faced with the injustice of a double lack that led to the disappearance of a subject who had never even been present in the eyes of the state, the Londres 38 Collective's urban intervention corrects this deficit of *absence*, multiplying the surplus of *effects-of-presence* in an artistic interpretation. The highly visible photos of José Huenante along the Alameda symbolically repaired the state of social invisibility in which both his existence – devalued by the state and its laws – and the case of his disappearance – ignored by the Military Justice department – had been submerged.[7]

The force of renewal of Londres 38's gesture consists in the move from the *already documented* cases of human rights violations under the dictatorship to the *undocumentation* of a case of police kidnapping in a supposed democracy. Thus, the Londres 38 Collective directed contemporary focus to the invisible mechanisms connecting the past and the present: the National Security Doctrine under the dictatorship and the neoliberal control of "public safety" in a democracy in conflict with the Mapuche people, whose communal organizations it persecutes. By examining how the past infiltrates the present under new, surreptitious forms of legality–illegality, this urban intervention, in addition to recalling the victimhood produced by the past dictatorship, also validates a new political critique of (anti-Mapuche) state violence in an era of democratic recovery.

The artist Camilo Yáñez's contribution to the Londres 38 urban intervention is a work titled "Aunque sea por un día" ["Even if only for a day"]. His artistic photographic enlargement replicates the layout of the front page of the daily newspaper *El Mercurio* but instead filled with photos of persons disappeared during the dictatorship, "even if only for a day," with the headline, "All of Chile Demands to Know Where They Are." This is an obviously fictitious headline, taking into account the newspaper's history of editorial support for the imperialist bourgeoisie's campaign against Unidad Popular, which goes back several years before Allende took office (all while receiving support from the United States' Central Intelligence Agency, which guaranteed that the subversive opposition would provoke a climate of ungovernability in Chile, later invoked as a justification for the 1973 military coup). It also reminds us that the *El Mercurio* editorial board never once spoke out against the human rights violations committed by Pinochet's military regime but instead acted in journalistic and commercial complicity with the apparatuses of state power. In the 2011 installation, Yáñez's work was located on the façade of the Iglesia de San Francisco, which is to say equidistant from both the Catholic University and the University of Chile. In August 1967, in the middle of a student-led university reform campaign, during the administration of Eduardo Frei Montalva, a banner was hung on the front of the Catholic University that read, "Chileans: *El Mercurio* Lies," in response to the attacks the conservative paper had launched against the student movement calling for university reforms. This phrase was forever imprinted on the collective imaginary until the most recent student movement, when another banner was hung in front of the University of Chile, with the new message invoking the earlier one and insisting on its clear relevance for the present: "Chileans: 40 Years Later *El Mercurio* Still Lies." The location of Yáñez's work on the Alameda associatively reunites a before (the "revolution in liberty" of Eduardo Frei Montalva's administration and university reform) and an after (post-democratic transition Chile and the student movement), endeavoring to prevent Salvador Allende's voice from being extinguished ("the great avenues will open again where free men will walk to build a better society") and simultaneously continuing to alert the public about *El Mercurio*'s ideological conservativism and editorial fraud, which have always obstructed any changes or reforms to the deceptive Constitution.

Yáñez's redesigned front page is implausible because of the newspaper's widely known history of systematically denying the existence of human rights violations during the military administration. The critical and artistic simulation of an *El Mercurio* front page with photographs of the disappeared under the headline "All of Chile Demands to Know Where They Are" orients the public's attention toward the past so that they will remember how *El Mercurio* habitually covered up the dictatorship's crimes with silence and false reports. It

Image 6: Tribute to José Huenante, 2011, Commemoration Ceremony for the International Day of the Disappeared. Artwork by Camilo Yáñez installed on the façade of the Iglesia de San Francisco, Avenida Bernardo O'Higgins, Santiago de Chile. Photo © Camilo Yáñez Studio (courtesy of Camilo Yáñez).

accomplishes this by using art to frame a present-day denunciation in order to publicly humiliate the newspaper for its past shame (which its editorial board continually tries to sweep under the carpet). Yáñez's work rhetorically contrasts the yesterday that was left unsaid by the newspaper with the confession of today through art, which serves as the public's critical consciousness, exhibiting the portraits of identified victims as photographic evidence of the lies promoted by the false headlines that covered up past events.[8] By generating a semantic dissociation between discourse and reality in this satirical *El Mercurio* front page, Yáñez's work encourages suspicion about the veracity of the stories the newspaper currently publishes. The work "Aunque sea por un día" offers symbolic reparations to the victims' families by forcing the paper that distorted death and disappearance to display the photographic presentation of these identities that now suddenly reappear on the front page of the same paper that denied they ever existed. Yáñez's photographic enlargement also displays the satirical newspaper on a table, accompanied by a cup of coffee and eyeglasses. During the dictatorship, *El Mercurio* was delivered to subscribers' homes with the slogan "*El Mercurio* is a daily necessity," thus insinuating itself into the everyday lives of its readers, reiterating the ideological message that it should be consumed "daily" in order to achieve greater social bearing in a society rife with censorship. The bourgeois table where *El Mercurio* subscribers would sip their morning coffee has its painful counterpart in another (for these subscribers, unimaginable) table: a breakfast table, fixed in the memories of the victims' families as the last memory of a time shared at home with the disappeared before they were gone forever. In Yáñez's work, the coffee table and its censored inverse (the breakfast table of the disappeareds' families) evoke the home life split in two by the antagonistic experiences of those who, on the one hand, were situated on the side of the perpetrators and accepted false news stories and those who, on the other hand, occupied the place of the victims and were relegated by *El Mercurio* to public irrelevance. By staging *the private* (the domesticity and everydayness of the coffee or breakfast table) in *the public* realm of the city, Yáñez's work composes a form of "public transit" that brings the suspected truth to be put on display in the street as a revealed truth.

Yáñez's work illustrates another incredible turn of history that also takes on the symbolic value of reparation and consolation. Agustín Edwards, owner of *El Mercurio*, and Eliodoro Matte, owner of Empresas CMPC (commonly known as "*la Papelera*"), put together – in their capacity as powerful businessmen – multiple illegal associations that first conspired against the Unidad Popular government and then benefited from the economic advantages given to them during the country's neoliberal refounding during the Pinochet era.[9]

La Papelera and *El Mercurio* defended the monopoly on wealth forged by the illegal privatization efforts of large businesses favored by the military dictatorship. A good part of this wealth was accumulated in the logging industry, led by the Matte clan and *la Papelera*, including the latter's declared alliance with *El Mercurio*.[10] The logging industry was subsidized by the same military government that displaced and appropriated the lands of indigenous communities in the Araucanía region (where José Huenante was from) for their timber plantations. On Yáñez's simulated front page of *El Mercurio*, next to the photographs of the disappeared, there is an editorial written about the disappearance of a Mapuche youth. Yáñez's work obliges *El Mercurio* to renounce – "even if only for a day" – its campaign to extinguish its hostile memory and convert its pages into a community of solidarity that, through art, removes José Huenante from the pain of his solitude and abandonment. Yáñez's work figuratively restores to Huenante – "even if only for a day" – a form of control over his identity through which he can reconquer territory (in the newspaper) that the logging industry had taken from his community through the devastation of forests and the dispossession of the Mapuche people from their lands to enrich the neoliberal state under the protection of the military regime. The critical and artistic reterritorialization of Huenante's photo in the hegemonic place of the front page of *El Mercurio*, whose structures of economic and political power had previously condemned him to nonexistence, now grants this new victim – "even if only for a day" – the symbolic compensation of status and position. Yáñez brings the non-place of the disappeared Huenante to the prime location of a front-page headline, allowing a Mapuche subject deprived of his lands to recuperate something of them in the national paper of record as a floating signifier of the identities that remain displaced, discarded, oppressed, and suppressed in Chile today. Yáñez's art imaginatively repairs the damages caused by *El Mercurio*'s corporate power by representing on a large scale an act of citizen justice that, through the symbolic operations of condensation and transference, produces an imaginary of loss and the reparation of damages.

The Londres 38 Collective's intervention broke the rituality of commemoration (paying tribute to the disappeared) exposed to the dangers of being reified in the remote past, dislocating its familiar codes of memory by short-circuiting images, places, and times. Generating cuts and discontinuities in the line of the historical transmission of memory, Londres 38 reactivated what had been buried in memory about human rights violations by initiating changes of *effects* and *affects*. This gesture allowed the unrecognized (the omitted, the distorted, the negated) to take on an expressive voice – in the form of an interruption – in the circuit of public discourse. It inverted the official media's condemnation of the disappeared to a position of enunciative lack. In turn, the artwork and its multivocality of meaning transformed non-identity as *subtraction* (José Huenante) into a *symbolic excess* that compensated for the damage of lack and absence with an intensive and prolific multiplicity of marks of presence saturated with allegories and metaphors.

It is important to note that the Londres 38 Collective's intervention on the International Day of the Disappeared in 2011 was not unanimously endorsed by the community of victims' families, who were divided into those who felt that using the image of someone who was disappeared in democratic Chile distorted (betrayed) the commemorative value of the past victims of the dictatorship, and those who wagered on the transfiguration of the historical memory of the dictatorship through displacements of context that would amplify and renew its capacity for public dialogue. What was at stake in the Londres 38 working group's internal discussion was strategic: the counterpoint between, on the one hand, a contemplative vision of memory (that of the mimetic repetition of a literal past) and, on the other, the performativity of a critical, transformative memory that unsettles the known past in order to liberate new emancipatory forces of

meaning through interferences, controversies, and antagonisms regarding the evaluative significance of memory.

9

Media Explosion of Memory in September 2013

While recognizing the progress that has been made with regard to the "politics of memory" in Chile (the denunciation of crimes against humanity and the measures taken to address truth, justice, and reparations), Steve J. Stern asks the following question: "Have we achieved a renewal capable of reaching the unconvinced and the youth of the future? Does memory still have the capacity to reach younger generations who have already accepted the truth of the occurrence of atrocious and morally reprehensible human rights violations?"[1] September 2013 – the month of the fortieth anniversary of the military coup – constituted a trial by fire for these questions, which evaluate the capacity for the political and social renewal of the persuasive force of the discourse of memory in Chile. The occasion of crossing the generational threshold of forty years undoubtedly provoked consideration of new strategies for transmitting the historical memory of the military coup as a recollection that continues to grow more distant in time, especially for those who did not directly live it. This generational threshold signaled in some way a change of scenery from memory (the direct experiences of the victims or witnesses of traumatic events) to what some theorists call "postmemory"[2] – the universe of thematizations that indirectly extend to the entire chain of references and interpretations of memory through versions of versions, images of images, stories of stories that are each time further from their historical origins. In September 2013, in contrast to previous commemorations of the military coup, it was mass media that played the leading role in the explosion of social memory in the transmission of archives, testimonies, and interviews in print and on the screen – a series of episodes from which we should recover some montages of meaning in particular.

Traces and the archive: the last time ...

What is a trace of memory? It is the inscription left by an event on the foundation of a perceptive and imaginative retention that makes memory more durable. A trace is the intermittent signal that is engraved on the surface as a feature or vestige of the experience of the past. The trace is, on the one hand, the (inscribed, engraved) mark that records memory, and, on the other, the potential for reanimating the past that has been deposited in this reserve – a potential which keeps it prepared for any future advent of memory. The trace is a key signifier in Freudian analysis, in which the genealogy of psychical memory has encoded in the trace the functions of inscription, superimposition, erasure, and the peeling back of the mnemic layers that intervene in memory. However, the theme of the trace has also become constitutive of the contemporary problematic known as the archive, which we understand to be the storage apparatus for the material remnants that registered the event, with the intent of conserving them and protecting them from disappearance and forgetting. The documents in archives safeguard and transmit the memory of the historical event and serve the discipline of history by accumulating evidence and clues that can help to corroborate the truth of what happened. However, the theme of the archive has already exceeded the borders of the discipline of history to expand itself as a *corpus* of public memory in communication societies where historical events are disseminated around the globe by means of technologies designed to maximally extend the reach of their reproductive traces. The capacity of archives to retain and preserve documentary evidence guarantees that the trace will endure in a technological prolongation of the past that seeks to allow future viewers to relive an experience that has already happened and thus appears to be irretrievably gone. The inextricability of the elements of the chain *event–recording–reproduction–transmission*, which defines the archive and its problematic, bears an ambiguity toward times and modes (past–present, closeness–distance, disappearance–reappearance, original–copy) that causes the traces of the past to oscillate between loss (what already was, what ceased to exist as something unrepeatably *alive* in its first instance) and restitution (the supplement of technical duration that saves the dead time of the already-was from oblivion, multiplying the effects of its republication into an infinite series). Every reproduction of the archive is faced with this dilemma of the dead–living of a historical and biographical time whose experience is fraught with the melancholia of mourning in spite of its reparative role as a technological substitute. This is because this so-called substitute can never assuage the sorrow of renunciation and loss associated with the unrepeatability of the *already-was*.

One of the many television programs broadcast in September 2013, *11 íntimo* (The 11th Up-Close and Personal) on Canal 13, recreated the experiences of individuals who were directly involved in the events of September 11, 1973, focusing on two witnesses who discuss the visual and auditory traces they themselves recorded as a reminder of a "last time" that had a double ending: the defeat of the dream of Unidad Popular (the bombing of La Moneda) and Salvador Allende's death in the presidential palace. Manuel Martínez (camera operator for Televisión Nacional) and Leonardo Cáceres (news director for Radio Magallanes) were both carrying out their professional duties on that day and thus witnessed this final moment. The first individual, Martínez, recorded the last living image of Allende standing on the balcony of La Moneda:[3] Salvador Allende looking out onto the horizon (perhaps with an indecipherable burden of meditative regret?) at 8:00 a.m. and greeting the small number of passersby a few hours before the midday bombing attack, when the coup had already begun to unleash its fury but before its true extent was clear. Martínez remarked: "That morning of September 11, I arrived at work at 7 in the morning when suddenly my boss called me and said 'Go

over to La Moneda. There's some saber-rattling going on ...'
We started to check things out there ... Dr. Allende came
outside to look ... and that was what I was able to record.
He was on the balcony, and that was the last time I saw
him."⁴ Cáceres, the second individual, produced the radio
broadcast of Allende's final speech, delivered at 10:00 a.m.
in his chambers in La Moneda, in which he bade farewell to
the people of Chile shortly before taking his own life. Radio
Magallanes was the only Leftist radio station that continued
to broadcast after all the other stations' antennas had been
destroyed by bombs, Cáceres recalls: "At Radio Magallanes
we were all working very hard, we knew that we were living
at what could be a decisive moment. We were so strongly
committed to continuing to broadcast, we kept calling on
the people to resist. And I was absolutely convinced that
those who carried out the coup were only one part of the
Armed Forces. Then someone said to me, 'Leonardo, I have
the President on the line. Make an announcement.' So, I
said: 'And now, here on Radio Magallanes, the President of
the Republic, Dr. Salvador Allende, will address the workers
of the nation from the presidential palace ... .' At 10:20 or
10:30 a.m. our radio transmission was suddenly cut off."⁵

These two witnesses of history, Martínez and Cáceres,
recorded with two different means of capturing images and
sounds what turned out to be the final repositories of the
(visual and auditory) traces of a past whose tragic *already-
was* has managed to endure in the *still-is* of the image and
sound that have preserved the effect of the physical and vocal
presence of Salvador Allende up to the present. In *11 íntimo*,
Martínez and Cáceres, witnesses of their own past, are filmed
in a sequence in which they are asked to view (on a television
screen) and to listen (on a cassette player-recorder) once again
to what they themselves recovered as a sublime remainder of
a moment forever marked by Allende's death and by the
consequent disappearance of both his physical image and the
grain of his voice. The qualitative leaps in technology and
equipment between, on the one hand, the past in which the
traces were recorded (September 11, 1973) and, on the other,
the present of their rebroadcast forty years after the coup as
televisual archives, which position Martínez and Cáceres as
witnesses to their own achievements, highlight the abyss that

separates the unique, original moment of the historical event from its subsequent reproduction. The melancholic visages of Martínez and Cáceres, reliving the memory of September 11, 1973 in *11 íntimo*, acknowledge this phantasmatic gap between presence and absence, experience and recreation – a gap that is still remembered with the help of technological prostheses but which, unfortunately, cannot prevent media artificiality from erasing the emotion of a living being, of the first person, of unique experience, of events authentically lived in real time. Martínez watches a digital television screen, seeing once again the images that his reporter's camera furtively captured of a defenseless Allende on the balcony of the presidential palace – an Allende who was unprotected from the threatening contingency that was going to end in his death – just before he would definitively pass into history as myth and legend. For his part, Cáceres listens again, forty years after the military coup, to Allende's speech, which, due to his technical and professional dedication, was saved for posterity in a radio recording; a speech whose majestic tone continues to resound into the present as the comrade president's interminable farewell, which was broadcast to future generations thanks to the recorded archives of memory. The passage of forty years between these two scenes, a period of historical time that was not only permeated by different political and social processes but also by various technological changes with regard to image and sound, scans the memory of history as these two witnesses melancholically relive Allende's "last time." The memory of the history lived by Martínez and Cáceres is torn apart and torn between the experience of an irrecoverable loss (the broken dreams of Unidad Popular and the sacrificial death of Allende, who embodied them) and the technological recovery of those traces of his image and voice, which seal the tragic event of the breaking of history with a citation (an iteration, a deferral) that is forever rebroadcast as the mourning of loss.

The bombing of La Moneda

Ever since audiovisual reproduction technology has existed, not only have media outlets felt the obligation to cover all events destined to be considered as such by history but also, at this point, nothing ever becomes an event without this media coverage, which projects it into the communicative sphere of the information society. Nowadays, no historical event exists outside the reach of the technologies that have been designed to disseminate it and expand its audiovisual archives. Thus, one cannot but associate the 1973 coup in Chile with the filmed footage of the bombing of La Moneda, which is broadcast during every commemorative cycle. The same images, over and over again: the Hawker Hunter fighter-bomber jets initiating the attack from the air, the military tanks surrounding the Palacio de La Moneda, the flames consuming its walls and windows, the Chilean flag on fire above the palace... . In spite of the thorough declassification of photographic and audiovisual archives from September 1973 (motivated by the fortieth anniversary of the coup), it is striking that this same footage of the bombing of La Moneda is nearly always repeated time and again to document the event: the same preferential angle (from the windows of what was at that time the Hotel Carrera on the Plaza de la Constitución) and the same anguished view of the progress of the military's destruction of the palace as a republican symbol of democratic life; the same simultaneous framing and absence of a "point of view" (only something like a faint absence of the intentionality of meaning) in this stunned and distraught recording of the event, intuiting that the images would serve as undeniable filmic evidence that everything occurred "as it is" before they were repeated in multiple versions. The footage of the bombing of La Moneda is the technological means that verify the truth of such an unimaginable act. The objectivity of the material filmed by the camera that day serves to correct any future memory that would seek to diminish the severity of what *really* happened. Although the images of La Moneda in flames barely show the shocked gazes of witnesses who happened to be present and who clearly could not believe what they were seeing, this footage recorded for all time the incontrovertible fact of the violence of the military attack on the presidential palace. Since then, the *already-was* of this final image of La Moneda in flames became an overdetermining factor in historical recollection of the 1973 military coup, proving, as

Georges Didi-Huberman has argued, that "the image is the eye of history: its tenacious function [is] making visible."[6] The images of the bombing of La Moneda, recorded for posterity, are irrefutable evidence of *how* the real catastrophe took place.

The insistence and persistence of this footage of the burning of La Moneda on September 11, 1973 fulfills the first requirement for public attention formulated by Susan Sontag: "Creating a perch for a particular conflict in the consciousness of viewers exposed to dramas from everywhere."[7] The abysmal fixed image of the façade of La Moneda in flames is the "viewpoint" of the historical consciousness whose gaze is fixed by the event of the coup in Chile: a coup overthrowing the democratic life that dislocated time from the historical continuity in which *before* and *after* could no longer be returned to the passive order of a simple chronology of occurrences.

Every time the same images of that September day appear on (invade) the screen, they reproduce the same stupefied gaze that cannot believe what it is seeing: La Moneda being attacked by Chilean Air Force bombers. This symbolic image, having been broadcast around the world a thousand times, must struggle against the complacency of the repetition effect that ends up weakening the intensity of any memory. One single image reiterated *ad infinitum* (La Moneda in flames) that, nevertheless, has its perceptual material altered every time technological advances relocate it from one archival medium to another, especially if one takes into account that "the image is already transformed with every act of visualization using a different, new technology."[8] The archival explosion of programs on every Chilean television network in September 2013 marked the beginning of the technological reprocessing of these historical images of the bombing, which has passed through multiple phases of the inscription and transcription of its original sources to the latest media formats, which reactivate the traces of memory through audiovisual technology. These media, which range from the analog photography of the past to the digital reproduction of the present, inevitably combine originals and copies in a confusion of registers and exhibit a trans-mediality that constitutes an affective distance that separates the indexicality of the historical time in which the original footage was shot (the first view of the bombed palace that produces the traumatic effect of the shock of history) from what came afterward: images of the military coup that were duplicated and processed with post-production touch-ups that could never cover over the void left by this historic loss of life. Despite these touch-ups using the latest technology, the image of the Palacio de la Moneda in flames continues to be an allegory of the idea of "images that burn" explored by Didi-Huberman: "One cannot speak of the contact between image and the real without speaking of a kind of conflagration. Therefore, one cannot speak of images without speaking of ashes."[9] In spite of the infinite technological reprocessing of its multiple copies, the image of La Moneda in flames continues to burn, just as its original burning and ashes will always cause us to mourn.

It is noteworthy that the only other visual footage of catastrophe that competes on an international level with the iconic repetition and saturation of the bombing of La Moneda on September 11, 1973 in Santiago is the attack on the Twin Towers of the World Trade Center in New York City carried out on another September 11, this time in 2001. For many witnesses of the New York attack, the sensation of confronting the inassimilable experience of "the *seeing* ... dislocated from the *knowing*" that overtakes any ability to understand could have been similar to what the witnesses of the bombing of La Moneda experienced.[10] The image of La Moneda in flames was the only footage recorded that day (and thus it was the only editable footage) due to the censorship the dictatorship imposed from the very beginning of the coup. In contrast, the massive circulation of the same images of the Twin Towers stems not from being the product of a military dictatorship's censorship but rather because of how vision in general today is standardized by "the effects of globalization on the market of images and therefore on representations of reality" that massively select and condition perspectives.[11] The images of La Moneda under attack in Chile and of the Twin Towers falling in New York are secretly related to one another through an accursed connection between the United States and Latin America (e.g., US intervention in the preparations for the military coup in Chile – whose earlier September 11 refuses to be occluded by a later tragedy coinciding with it) as both events produced death and sorrow in their respective countries. The globalization of these two images of disaster can even be read as a perverse game. It is as if the global dissemination of images of the Twin Towers' destruction, always framed in terms of the unprecedented scale of its horror, is meant to communicatively deny the US's will to domination by robbing the memory of the Chilean coup of its role in history by situating it as one date competing with another. By wanting to displace the bombing of La Moneda from the foreground of collective memory in order to replace it with images of the World Trade Center attack, it would seem as if North American globalization were waging a second "coup" (this time through the media) against the memory of the Chilean military coup, perhaps to try to conceal the unbreakable bond that led to the US's secret intervention and collaboration in the destruction of democracy and the establishment of the military dictatorship in Chile.

Sontag formulated a second requirement for winning the public's attention through images of disaster which invokes the need for the "diffusion and rediffusion of snippets of footage about the conflict"[12] so as not to waste the power of the image, which must remain unique in the face of the indifference/indifferentiation of the general. According to Sontag, it is necessary to reinforce the singularity of a penetration of visual memory that accompanies the sequence of individual and collective circumstances that highlight its unmistakable particularity, separating it from the other "wars happening elsewhere," competing with one another to spectacularize tragedy for audiences around the world. In light of this argument, we should recall that the first time we saw the semi-clandestine copies of the footage of the bombing of La Moneda – as a magisterial image inserted into a narrative with monumental intrigue woven around the multiple "snippets of footage about the conflict" – was in Patricio Guzmán's documentary *La batalla de Chile*. However, in September 2013, a zone of blindness prevented us from seeing what should have jumped right out at us: the way in which the repeated images of La Moneda in flames (shown on all television programs commemorating the fortieth anniversary of the coup) systematically avoided any reference to Guzmán's documentary, which was the first to show these epic, historical images. Chilean television made it seem as if no one knew that the cinematic narrative of *La batalla de Chile* continues to be the most complex reflection of all filmic attempts to interpret Unidad Popular and the coup. This zone of blindness, which occurred in September 2013, clouded over an obligatory question: why, after the dictatorship has ended and the country has begun its transition to democracy, has *La batalla de Chile* been held hostage by a public television network (Televisión Nacional: the self-proclaimed "network for all Chileans"), which, despite having acquired the rights to the film, refuses to broadcast or exhibit it in any way? Perhaps it is due to precisely the same reason evoked by Sontag (the need for the "diffusion and rediffusion of snippets of footage of the conflict"), only with its critical sense inverted. The fear of the reactivation of meaning, which was widespread during the Transition, perhaps has to do with the fact that *La batalla de Chile* was able to bring the historical contingency of Unidad Popular's one-thousand-day-long administration to its highest political expression, recreating in each fold of history the disconnections of meaning that the sequence of events was forced to confront, and making it so that, forty years later, viewers can have the opportunity to exercise their historical imagination and freely reconnect the "snippets of footage about the conflict" so that the "official memory" is unable to order them "correctly."

The cut of *La batalla de Chile* that Guzmán made from exile is composed of a three-part story consisting of "The bourgeois insurrection," "The coup," and "Popular power." The director makes use of an exceptional authorial device of chronological insubordination, which designates the third and final part of the film as "Popular power" rather than "The coup," as an order loyal to sequential history would have dictated. It is this audacious device of chronological insubordination that allows Guzmán to present the hopeful memory of the history of Unidad Popular as not completely destroyed by the factual triumph of the 1973 coup. Because of this alteration of historical sequence, which changes the temporal order of the actual sequence of events, *La batalla de Chile* makes it so that the insubordinate corporeal machine of the revolutionary Allende era ("Popular power") continues to detonate its explosive charge of aspirations and uprisings even after having been crushed by the military coup. Perhaps this subversive mode of temporalizing memory is capable of inverting the relation between the past, the present, and the future, a memory still considered dangerous by those who control Chilean media and continue to enforce a virtual censorship of *La batalla de Chile*. Disobeying the closure of a completed past, the time machine that is *La batalla de Chile* keeps the past potential for rebellion alive ("Popular power") so that this insurrectionary past will continue to cross over into our present–future with its transformational energies.

Strategies of memory, the power of images, and media control

There were several programs broadcast on Chilean television during the month of September 2013 that appealed to the intersubjective and transgenerational dimension of memory. In the case of Televisión Nacional, two stand out: *El año que cambió nuestras vidas* [The year that changed our lives], based on the stories of "five Chilean families with different experiences in conversation about the events of September 11, 1973, reflecting forty years later on how the coup changed our lives. Five families have made the decision to dare to talk about what has been kept in silence for forty years";[13] and *La voz de los 40* [The voice of 40], which featured interviews with "people who are 40 years old and were thus born in 1973, when the country was rocked by the coup. Their testimonies tell of how Chilean history and its legacy are intertwined with an indelible mark ... What are the events that marked the generation of '73? What memories do they have of the worst institutional disaster in Chilean history? How were they able to overcome these birthmarks, and how do they view Chile today?"[14]

In *El año que cambió nuestras vidas*, the memory of the military coup and dictatorship is recreated within the framework of the family (among parents, nieces and nephews, siblings, or grandchildren), sharing experiences of the time along with information about their lives – photo albums, letters, etc. – which help transfer memory from one generation to another, provoking curiosity from family members about unexpected details of the life stories featured in the program. The other program, *La voz de los 40*, is an investigative report on how the military coup and dictatorship affected the lives of those who were born in 1973 through a series of interviews with figures including the grandsons of both Augusto Pinochet and Salvador Allende, mixing family and politics throughout the course of their respective lives. What both programs have in common is an obvious concern that their contents reflect the "different sensibilities" which, according to the Televisión Nacional board of directors, coexist in Chile, seeking a balanced – proportionate – focus on the revision of the historical context of memories of the military coup. That is to say, balance here is the search for the "fair" middle ground between extremes that are clearly manifested in the choice of the witnesses who lived through the era and who come from diametrically opposed backgrounds: families from the Right and families from the Left, as if an objective view of the military coup – Televisión Nacional, which calls itself the "network of all Chileans" claims to represent this objectivity – could be naturally derived from the noncontradictory sum of two visions of the past which are presumed to be simply *different from* rather than *in direct conflict with* one another. Both of these programs privilege the individual–singular over the collective–general by recollecting the traumatic past through a framework shaped by the biographical circumstances of how each kind of family was affected by the crisis of 1973, almost going so far as to bracket off all historical antagonisms. As Rodrigo Moreno, the director of *El año que cambió nuestras vidas*, explains: "the idea is to show families who allow us to connect emotionally with the era and all of its truths. There is no judgment of history, or of the families here. We will be faithful to each family's story."[15]

The search for balanced perspectives that would "center" judgment of the past and consider experiences that oppose one another via the path of juxtaposition rather than of confrontation was also the journalistic strategy the Megavisión network pursued, as seen in the first episode of their series *Así viví el 11* [That's how I lived the 11th], which is titled

"Dos mujeres en cada lado de la trinchera" ["Two women from opposing trenches"]:

The front pages of the newspapers of September 8, 1973 reflected a seemingly out-of-control radicalization. Rumors of a military coup was the daily bread. Two women, who at that time were both young mothers and housewives, lived in a tense situation on opposing sides of the divisions that would mortally wound Chileans' ability to coexist ... Today we will focus on the story of these two women who, in 1973, had much in common: both were young mothers around 30 years of age, both of their husbands were important figures in their respective fields (one was a naval captain who would eventually become Commander-in-Chief of the Chilean Navy; the other was an engineer who served as a minister in the administrations of Allende, Lagos, and Bachelet). But that morning, both women were distraught because they had no idea what might happen to their husbands.

The ideological antagonism of the social projects that, in 1973, separated these two protagonists from "opposing sides" of political history was subsumed in the essentialist femininity of the woman–wife, based on a gender convention that, by actualizing the nature of these sentiments, highlighted their condition as "distraught women" and shifted the focus from the public realm to the private.

Chilevisión's program *Chile: Las imágenes prohibidas* [Chile: Forbidden images] – which had the highest ratings of September 2013 – wagered on a different communicative strategy:

Forty years have passed since the military coup, and there is still much that we do not know, stories and testimonies that have been silenced. Images that, during seventeen years of dictatorship, were prohibited from being broadcast and, after twenty-three years, continue to be forgotten. It is an unprecedented archive that we rescued from oblivion and made public for the first time. We reconstitute history from the efforts of those who photographed and filmed the history of the era and who were also the protagonists of those painful days. These images were seen around the world but were censored in Chile. Behind this imagery, we find people whose memory we keep alive today, even though their rawness still shocks us. These are the images we have tried to recover ... They are fragmented recordings, stories of the lives, pain, and deaths of anonymous Chileans who faithfully revealed what occurred here.

The point of view articulated by *Chile: Las imágenes prohibidas* openly condemns the military dictatorship's human rights violations without trying to balance this condemnation with explanations, which the Right always seems to require, of how the coup was a response to the exacerbation of hatred and the ruination of democracy caused by the Unidad Popular government. Across the span of four episodes, *Chile: Las imágenes prohibidas* openly expresses its solidarity with the victims of the repressive dictatorship. Defending its efforts to publicly reveal what at the time was still invisibilized as memory ("forty years have passed since the military coup, and there is still much that we do not know, stories and testimonies that have been silenced"), this program addresses the subject of intergenerational memory, putting into circulation unknown or insufficiently known materials that would agitate popular consciousness, especially among younger generations.

The historical, sociopolitical, and referential density of the audiovisual material in *Chile: Las imágenes prohibidas* and the emotional charge registered by its interviews with victims of military repression (including Estela Ortiz, Manuel Guerrero, Javiera Parada, and Carmen Gloria Quintana) undoubtedly contributed to expanding and reinforcing the field of social memory. This archived footage intensified memories of the years of military violence with a double wager on the power of images: an *authenticating* power (what is exhibited on the screen is perceived as having occurred as such because of the "truth"-effect of the documentary genre, which by the same token lends full credibility to the film's condemnation of the human rights violations of the dictatorship) and a *condemnatory* power (the abuses related in first-person by the victims themselves or by witnesses are so authentically serious that they cannot be justifiably rebuked). It is therefore not surprising that the Chilean Right and the media connected to it have reacted suspiciously, forty years after the coup, to the massive success of these visual archives as a resource for improving collective memory in its task of recalling the dictatorship's abuses, protesting that "we must put into question the problematic nature of images as sources for knowing the past."[16]

We could say that the images of the archive serve as evidence of the extent to which they indexically assign "what has been" (Roland Barthes) of a historical event through its apparatuses of capture and its exhibition of the real. All the same, images always need to be situated in a context of critical analysis of the different cultural patterns that organize its social meaning and interpretation in order to evaluate what is hidden behind the myth of the "objectivity" of technology as proof of reality. Neither the selectivity of the frame (What is included in the image and what is not? Which field of vision is privileged by it?), nor the intentionality of a point of view (What type of reaction does this evaluative perspective, which shapes the image's meaning, seek to provoke in the viewer?), nor the narrative quality of the scene (What kind of memory is produced by the story of the past being told to us and which shapes our recollection?) are ever innocent. In particular, if it is a matter of *vision*, then the *delimitation of the frame* – that is, the edges that separate the picture in which the images appear from its surroundings, as well as the lines drawn between the visible (the demonstrable) and the nonvisible (the hidden) that are enabled every day by dominant communication technologies – should be analyzed. It is this kind of semiotic, discursive, ideological, and cultural contextualization that most effectively contributes to a critique of memory when it comes to archival practices of the transmission of the past in order to interrogate its images with regard to strategies of omission and/or recovery that separate what is *on view* from what has been *removed from circulation*.

What is certain is that neither moral indignation in response to the abuses committed by the dictatorship's machinery of terror nor compassion for the victims of these abuses is enough to build a critical consciousness for the recollection of history. In addition, it is necessary to analyze the *edited* character of this recollection in order to understand more precisely its relation to the socio-communicative patterns of power used by dominant media outlets during the Chilean Transition. In the case of *Chile: Las imágenes prohibidas*, the force of *what is exhibited* (declassified and, up to that point, untelevised audiovisual archives) tended to inhibit any question about the reasons why these images remained *unexhibited* or *unexhibitable* for a long period during the democratic transition, long after all of the dictatorship's censorship had been lifted.

Chile: Las imágenes prohibidas includes in its episodes the perspectives and experiences of "those who photographed and filmed the dark story of those years" (Claudio Pérez, Kena Lorenzini, Raúl Cuevas, Pablo Salas, and others), who had the courage to confront censorship, violence, and repression during the dictatorship to document the regime's criminal abuses, which were systematically covered up and denied by a complicit media apparatus. *Chile: Las imágenes prohibidas* recognizes that "these images belong to the semi-clandestine news network Teleanálisis, which covered what the major networks of the time refused to show," referring to the dangerous conditions of producing the visible during the dictatorship. However, the success of *Chile: Las imágenes prohibidas* obfuscated the question of why, throughout twenty-three years of democracy, these images continued to be hidden away or held back by the media outlets of the Transition. The program failed to establish for a national audience any uncomfortable questions related not only to the historical *conditions of production* of such images during the dictatorship but also to the *conditions of recognition* that these images were denied during the Transition. The images of violence and repression recorded by the people interviewed in *Chile: Las imágenes prohibidas* usually found their journalistic homes in magazines like *Hoy, Cauce, Aspi*, or *Análisis*, which provided space for their visual testimonies. What happened to these opposition media outlets? Newscaster Patricio Bañados, after having been the emblematic face of the successful NO campaign of the 1988 plebiscite and then later completely absent from television screens during the Transition years, remarks that "it was in the media where the worst effects of the Concertación's betrayal could be found ... leaving all outlets that opposed the dictatorship (*La Época, Hoy, Fortín Mapocho, Análisis, Aspi, Cauce*) to die a slow death."[17] The censorship of the images of memory is also a consequence of how the influence of corporate interests in media is transmitted both indirectly through advertising and directly through the ideological framework that sealed the pact between economy and society made by the Transition administrations.

The successful broadcast of the previously hidden materials of *Chile: Las imágenes prohibidas* in September 2013 did not, however, provide any opportunity to look more closely at the rest of the visible in order to scrutinize certain images that were not actually *prohibited* but rather simply *tolerated*: images that, inexplicably, were granted the banal permissiveness of a lack of critical vigilance. For example, more than forty years after the military coup, journalist Pablo Honorato continues to dispatch his daily reports on the Canal 13 news, "from the Court of Justice," occupying the same halls where, during Pinochet's regime, he enjoyed a suspicious level of hospitality and quite cordially interviewed the sinister Military Prosecutor Fernando Torres and the ominous Attorney General Ambrosio Rodríguez – the same Pablo Honorato who spread disinformation about the execution of political prisoners, reporting on them instead as "confrontations between military forces and opponents of the regime."[18] Why has this return to the "scene of the crime" (Honorato continues to report, undisturbed, from the same courthouse as before) escaped attention, forty years after the military coup, as if it were simply any other anodyne image? The month of September 2013 exposed the lack of critical forms of justice capable of investigating the origins of the televised coexistence of, on the one hand, the revelation of images censored by the dictatorship in programs like *Chile: Las imágenes prohibidas*, which managed to cause conscious outrage and, on the other, the offensive repetition of a news report ("Pablo Honorato, from the Court of Justice"), made completely banal by daily broadcasts in spite of the fact that his journalistic brand is associated with the reprehensible memory of the disinformation and counter-information used by the military regime to cover up its crimes.

Testimonies, revelations, and anti-confessions

The testimonial turn in contemporary thought about the recent past has multiplied the stories that give voice to the biographical so that memory may carry the mark of experience associated with the use of the first person, in contrast to what happens with the neutered discourse of the third person, which history uses to support the objectivity of facts. The fortieth anniversary of the coup abounded with memoiristic accounts that recreated the life trajectories of its primary and secondary actors.

In a post-dictatorship context, the acts of memory formulated by testimonies and confessions have the merit of commemorating what criminal destruction had left unrecorded, thereby rescuing these voices from the inferno; by revealing the suffering, these acts become irrefutable proof of the horrors experienced during the dictatorship. The biographical and testimonial turn of the act of remembering weaves together stories that signify for the victims the overcoming of both forgetting (the erasure of experience) and unprocessed mourning (the lack of an elaboration of a memory that, because it has been blocked, cannot be integrated into new paths of experience and life awareness). Making these testimonies public not only allows victims and witnesses to heal their own personal suffering, but it also provides social history and memory with living proof that these subjects, who now have the power to speak, suffered with their own bodies the abominations of persecution and torture, all of which the dictatorial regime officially denied.

During the long years of the Chilean Transition, governed by the discourse of reconciliation, the rhetorical and political artifice of consensus was designed to formalize the reintegrated community of an "us" that would make the "democracy of agreements" functional. In the social and communicative landscape of the Transition years, the memory of the dictatorship's atrocities was basically confined to the reports of tribunals or human rights commissions without the voices of condemnation having access to a verbality that would be sufficiently sensitive to the register of *affect*. The wounded subjectivities of the victims of torture and repression were deprived of universes of meaning, excluded from expressive territories for publicly communicating the harm that continued to afflict them. After many long years of silence and omission, some of these stifled or disregarded victims' voices ("We the tortured were forgotten for a long time"[19]), finally, forty years after the coup, had the opportunity to tell their stories on national television.

The program *Mentiras verdaderas* [True lies] featured a series of lengthy interviews with various ex-detainees and torture victims, giving particular attention to the victims of the Tejas Verdes detention center:[20] Manuel Zarate, Feliciano Cerda, Olga Letellier, and Ana Becerra. These survivors of torture were grateful for the chance to appear on television and give their testimonies because this opportunity was for them something like a restoration of their identities: "I am so thankful for this program ... This way many comrades can also talk about what they experienced. I am no longer a second-class citizen. I am just another Chilean. Finally, you will believe that everything I said about what happened was true."[21]

However, we should note the ambivalence of the gesture of publicizing testimonies of certain limit-experiences like torture. This ambivalence exists, on the one hand, in the beneficial reparative effect of the victims' testimonies as well as in their value as evidence for recognizing the past (not only the *experiential* truth but also the *referential* truth of situations of extreme horror that public opinion cannot help but morally reject). On the other hand, there is also the danger that publicizing these extreme acts risks becoming a sensationalist transgression of moral decency due to the setting of the interview, which was entirely inappropriate – that is to say, it completely missed the solemn tone one would expect, given the serious nature of the confession. This can be seen, for example, in the overly-bright lighting, the colorful stage design, the inquisitive brusqueness of certain questions, or the background of the public's morbid curiosity about what could be perceived in the victims' feeble expressions. We must not let go of the following insight: the apparatuses of terror that the military regime applied to its victims served not only to strip them from their revolutionary paths in a massive operation of ideological extermination; it also reintegrated their docile bodies into the neoliberal offensive that, among other effects, uses the image-commodity to commercialize everything (expressions, emotions, feelings) in the competition for ratings. When these testimonies of torture are transferred from the realm of the private to the mediated public sphere, the victims' stories are not protected from being devoured by the triviality of the market for shock value.

One unavoidable, although somewhat outdated, reference for framing the series of testimonies of the surviving Tejas Verdes torture victims who shared their experiences in *Mentiras verdaderas* in September 2013 is undoubtedly Hernán Valdés's book *Tejas Verdes: Diario de un campo de concentración en Chile* [Tejas Verdes: Diary of a Chilean concentration camp], which was first published outside Chile in 1974. This was the first testimony dedicated not only to relating an experience of the personal suffering and humiliation of incarceration and torture in the Tejas Verde camp but also to denouncing the centralized system of repressive violence by presenting evidence of the secret and anonymous functioning of the system's criminal organizations. The literary texture of Valdés's testimonial voice is able to penetrate the gaps and holes of destruction, modulating the drama with a form of writing that intimately works as a means of survival against the forces of the annihilation of knowledge because of the way his writing preserves the language (as expressive substance and signifying capacity) of all the organic and bodily catastrophes experienced by the tortured subject. The solitude inherent to writing a testimony, sheltered in the retrospective and introspective search for meaning, consists of a situation that is very different from a soundstage in a television studio, such as the one on which *Mentiras verdaderas* was produced, in which the exhibitive pressure of a live and direct broadcast threatens to subject the victims' testimony to sensationalistic overdramatization.

The confirmational force of testimony (the certainty of the witness's voice in the present connected to the existing fidelity between what can be lived of a limit-experience and what can be said about it) is concentrated in the precision of the details that reinforce the truth-effect of the testimonial narrative. But while these details convey the precision of what was lived, they also can become motifs whose realism is exaggerated on television by different visual techniques that disconnect them from the signifying conjuncture of the sequence from which they emerge. The technological approaches of the medium of television usually throw details out of proportion and anecdotally exaggerate them in order to enhance their visual impact in the immediate foreground, thus sacrificing the safety of a correctly calculated distance (neither too near nor too far away) that makes it possible to protect what is being put on display. A certain hypervisibility of details in some of the stories of torture ends up violating the subject–object relation that must be protected by the proper distance of a comprehensive but noninvasive view. This risk was not always navigated with due precision in *Mentiras verdaderas*. Nevertheless, its sequence of testimonies about Tejas Verdes functioned publicly as major proof of the undeniable abuses committed in the first torture center utilized by the DINA under Manuel Contreras's command. The fact that this series of testimonies about Tejas Verdes aired a week after CNN's interview with Contreras (on September 10, 2013), in which the ex-DINA chief once again denied everything that was proved to have happened by the testimonies and judicial investigations, made his shameless denials all the more shocking on a political and social level.

The staging of CNN's interview with Contreras registered a complex tension. This tension included, on the one hand, the (journalistic) desire to add material (revelations, secrets, confessions) to the public knowledge of the dictatorship's abuses in order to lend further truth value to the awareness of these abuses' unforgivable severity. This existed in tension, on the other hand, with the media sensationalism of the interview as a journalistic achievement that did not uncover any new or relevant information – just the same lies as always. A few critical voices took on the task of analyzing the intricacies of the supposed "journalistic impact" of the Contreras interview:

> CNN Chile broadcast the interview *in extensor*, without editing it in order to preserve its "journalistic impact" and to beat TVN and Canal 13 to it. Thus, the network acted as a naive echo chamber for the views of a convicted criminal, despite the efforts of interviewers Mónica Rincón and Daniel Matamala to confront the truths established by courts and the Rettig and Valech Reports ... Why give violators of human rights the freedom of expression they denied to their victims? Why allow them the privilege of a television broadcast to continue mocking the murdered and disappeared and thus make things worse for their families?[22]

In fact, with Contreras's interview, we see an anti-confession that obliges us to pay the price once more of tolerating the systematic reliance on falsehood with which the ex-DINA chief scorned any ethical search for truth. On September 10, 2013, Contreras made several declarations to the nation: "The Rettig Report is absolutely false"; "I did not give orders to disappear anyone"; "Not a single person died in any DINA detention center"; "In DINA interrogations, we did not torture anyone" and so on.[23] Systematically refusing to share any information about how DINA operated during the most violent period of the repressive system, Contreras (sentenced to a total of 500 years for crimes against humanity) not only denied every established truth about human rights violations, including those established by truth and justice commissions and tribunal reports; he also pronounced these historical lies in the inflammatory and arrogant tone of someone who has no fear of anyone else: "I will not die in prison," he sarcastically affirms during the interview. The only consolation for the victims of this intolerable humiliation that passed as an interview (in which Contreras almost brags about being held in the Cordillera Prison, where the interview was recorded) was that it caused a series of reactions that unanimously condemned the pompous and defiant remarks of someone who, even for the Right, had fallen into disgrace. This interview with Contreras brought about the surprising political consequence of Chilean President Sebastián Piñera ordering the closure of the Cordillera Prison, arguing that his decision was based on the three criteria of "safeguarding the equality of all before the law, internal security, and ensuring the efficiency of the riot police" – and it only sharpened the conflicts within the Alianza por Chile, whose doctrinaire background had already been interpellated by the public's judgment of the dictatorship.[24] All this and much more occurred with the commemoration of the fortieth anniversary of the military coup in Chile and the media explosion of memory that it produced.

10
Commemoration of the 40th Anniversary of the Military Coup ... and Afterwards

We know that collective memory of the past is not the same as the fixed memory preserved in the archives that document history. Rather, it is the untying and retying of those knots of historical signification that, in the inquisitive curiosity of the present, do not allow the past to be arrested in a crystallized image but rather grant enough mobility and plasticity to critically re-elaborate this past. The commemoration of the fortieth anniversary of the military coup in Chile drew a massive line across the social and political field that altered various coordinates of the public's relation to memory and citizenship. However, this line was later displaced and replaced by the events in the national present that were so unexpected that the already recorded lexicon of memory and human rights was forced to account for changes in how certain signs from the past are read in the event that they are abruptly shaken by dislocating forces in the present. From sudden movements generated by these present rumblings there emerges a necessarily discontinuous genealogy of memory, full of interruptions and heterogeneities that compel combinations of the past (remembrance) and the present (the living act of remembering) toward unexpected social horizons.

History, memory, and countermemories

History and memory have the past in common as an object of investigation and a source of reminiscence. Both explore the past, whether through documents that corroborate the truth of events (history) or testimonies that evoke subjective and intersubjective experience (memory). Both are connected to a yesterday that, in the case of history, is constructed around the dates on which something occurred and which mark periods or distinguish between different eras. In the case of memory, this yesterday is blurred in the constellated recollections of what one has experienced first-hand or what others have communicated of their own memories. It is common for historians – who are even suspicious at times of the scientific-disciplinary regime that specializes in objectivizing historical proof – to mistrust the subjectivity of memory, which, by recreating sensations and perceptions via the imagination, changes the contours of the "reality of what happened" that these historians seek to verify with demonstrative rigor. However, the apparatuses of intelligibility of past events that guide the evaluation of historical documents are updated in the functioning of internal and external changes that are rampant both in the discipline itself today and in the sociopolitical environment into which history is inserted when its contributions are deemed to be of public benefit. The discipline of history cannot enter into dialogue with its own time if it is not open to the historicity of the social – which is to say, if it does not incorporate into its understanding of history the ways in which the memories of different identity formations (especially in the case of victims of traumatic events) are affirmed in symbols, images, and representations that cause collective subjectivity to recognize itself in selective versions of the past, which, as fractured versions, will be debated and criticized by other, different, or contrary versions in endless wars over memory. The intersection of history and memory prevents the production of knowledge about the past from becoming disconnected from the social body in which subjects articulate their experiences of the transference and mediation of memory in their multiple interactions with the networks of public discourse that communicate and broadcast always updated versions of this past.

One decisive proof of the supposed scientific-professional vocation of a pure history (which is by definition suspicious of how the public sphere precariously interferes in the academic stronghold of the discipline of history) is the death of Augusto Pinochet in December 2006, which provoked a confrontation between social memory and the discipline of history.[1] Some rightward-leaning historians opined in the national press that Pinochet's death would open up the situation to the science of history so that the discipline would be able to evaluate the transcendence of his legacy and thereby produce a disinterested verdict about him. These historians effectively assumed that a greater distance from the immediacy of the present would generate an objective judgment removed from the passions that cloud reason and diminish the impartiality of scientific pronouncements on history: a history which, according to them, was impeded from being calmly deliberated while Pinochet, still alive, continued to polarize the country along a dichotomous axis of good and evil, which produced both love and hatred. The Right wagered that Pinochet's death would distance historians from the vicissitudes of the present atmosphere, and they particularly hoped that it would immunize history from the meddling of a social memory that had *subjectively* opposed the dictator and supported the victims of repression, leading "the Left" to claim hegemony over the story of the past. However, this was not the case. The death of Pinochet did not clear the way for a more "balanced" perspective on him, as is demonstrated by the way his controversial memory converted the occasion of the fortieth anniversary of the military coup into an endless series of debates on memory – all with a force that was inversely proportional to the Right's attempts to impose "objectivity" on any historical analysis of the military regime – which, according to them, should be able to distinguish between the "positive" (modernizing advances and the economic boom under the dictatorship's neoliberal paradigm) and the "negative" (human rights violations, which some qualified as mere individual excesses). On the contrary, as the dictatorship's archives were opened up to critical review and new investigations, it became increasingly clear how methodically the military apparatus's repressive designs were interwoven with the savage implementation of the free-trade-based market economy dictated by the Chicago School.[2] This methodical assemblage tells us that the terror inflicted on the enemies of the military regime through persecution, torture, and disappearance was the indispensable condition on which the military government's economists designed their neoliberal techniques and, with the help of state terrorism, relied on the obedience of subjects who were either anesthetized by fear or dazzled by the fascination of consumption that kept them in thrall to the fiction of Chile as a neoliberal paradise. In contrast to what conservative historiographers still desire, it has been amply demonstrated that Pinochet, as president of the military junta, served as the implacable link between the two (today indissociable) sides of the historical narrative of the military regime's cruelty. The ex-dictator, who died in December 2006 without ever having been punished for the crimes he committed, was the same man who ordered ex-director of the DINA, Manuel Contreras, to organize and carry out acts of repression. He was the same man who stripped the Chilean people of their sovereignty through the authoritarian 1980 Constitution and who applied a massive and brutal current of neoliberal shock therapy to the nation in an effort to reorient social subjectivities toward the compulsory commodification of social life.

The commemoration of the coup's fortieth anniversary vehemently restaged the debate between history and memory/ memories, bringing various historians, including Sergio Villalobos, Patricia Arancibia, Gabriel Salazar, and Alfredo Jocelyn Holt, to the court of mass media in order to compare their analyses of the varying circumstances surrounding the 1973 coup: the ideological polarization of the Cold War era and the virulent anti-Marxism unleashed by the phantoms of class struggle; the revolutionary utopias of Latin America and the defense of armed struggle as a means to destroy imperialism and take hold of power; the Chilean Right's fear of the people finally taking charge of their own destiny in a sustained struggle against exploitation, driven by Unidad Popular. This fortieth anniversary caused historians to reflect on the public uses of memory when its explosion in mass media demanded expert knowledge to engage with the collective excesses of the archives and testimonies of the past of Unidad Popular, the coup, and the military dictatorship – all of which saturated every media outlet in 2013.

For some historians, like Villalobos, the staging of the memory of the military coup and dictatorship at the Museum of Memory and Human Rights since its creation in 2010 distorts Chilean history in two senses.[3] First, it favors a tendentious view of the events, institutionally taking the side of the dictatorship's victims without countering this accusatory, partisan view (a version which identifies the Left as the symbolic owner of the memory of victimhood) with the opposite view (implicitly or explicitly embodied by the Chilean Right), thus creating an imbalance of historical justice with regard to this sequence of events. Second, because it expounds on a truncated history that began with the military coup of 1973 without incorporating the contextual background of the Unidad Popular era, the crisis of which would explain (according to Villalobos) the inevitability of the political and institutional break as a fatal consequence of a destructive, prior exacerbation of existing antagonisms which should be taken into account. In response to the historiographical demand for a chronological sequence that would go back and explain the causes of the military coup in order to restore to wholeness a less partisan account that would paint a more "complete picture," the defenders of the Museum of Memory and Human Rights correctly noted that the museum does not have as its objective the scientific explanation of a historical chain of causes and effects but, rather, the promotion of an ethical consciousness that morally condemns the horrors of the dictatorship so that Chileans will endorse the categorical imperative of "Never again!"[4]

However, when it comes to memory, we should remember that no institutional narrative of the past is safe from the ravages of submemories and countermemories that come into conflict over a narrative's meaning (however much this narrative may condemn human rights violations and speak out in defense of its victims) with a will to linearity and closure that is perceived as hegemonic by those who are excluded from its order. The dedication of this public building should have been the culmination of an itinerary that would cause the Museum of Memory and Human Rights to be seen as proof of the maturity of a citizenry that is now able to look upon the past and peacefully learn from its mistakes with the aim of not repeating them, thus reinforcing Chile's fledgling democracy with a solid institutional repudiation of human rights violations. The Museum of Memory initiative began to take shape during Michelle Bachelet's first administration (2006–10). Bachelet, whose father was tortured and died at the hands of the military dictatorship and who is herself an ex-militant and socialist who was also arrested by the Pinochet regime and later exiled, was the Minister of Defense in Ricardo Lagos's administration. This appointment was an allegorical representation of the national reunion between the victims of the dictatorship and the military institution that was meant to officially symbolize the end of the Transition. Bachelet's own political biography embodied the discourse of *memory as reconciliation*, which is the idea that memory represents society's reencounter with itself in an integrative frame of understanding that, looking toward the future, necessarily causes these convergences to overcome antagonisms in the name of the supreme good of democratic coexistence.

With four Concertación presidents in attendance – including Patricio Aylwín (1990–94), Eduardo Frei (1994–2000), Ricardo Lagos (2000–06), and Michelle Bachelet (2006–10) – the official inauguration ceremony for the Museum of Memory and Human Rights in January 2010 was an attempt to reinforce the progress of truth, justice, and reparations as signs of Chile's progressive restitution toward a full awareness of its past, which, in spite of its divided character, could now finally step into the public sphere of social recognition. As Bachelet herself declared on that day: "The inauguration of this Museum is a powerful sign of the strength of a united nation. A unity that is founded in a commitment to never return to the suffering of a tragedy like the one that happened here, which we will always remember." However, Bachelet's speech at the inauguration of the Museum of Memory and Human Rights was interrupted by two protesters – Catalina Catrileo, the sister of murdered Mapuche activist Matías Catrileo, and Ana Vergara Toledo, the sister of Rafael and Eduardo Vergara Toledo, who were murdered by agents of the dictatorship – who scaled a light pole in the central courtyard where the ceremony was being held.[5] Both women demanded justice for the violation of rights suffered by the Mapuche people due to the institutionalized politics of the Concertación administration. The Mapuche protest movement emerged with a denunciative force that was not included in the Museum's institutional booklet (Catalina Catrileo shouted from the top of the light pole: "I am the sister of Matías Catrileo, murdered by your government, President Bachelet!") and which pushed for the frame of reference of the term "human rights" to also include a fragment of social memory that had been unjustly excluded from the symbolic lexicon of the dictatorship's victims. Protesting against this exclusion and segregation of subaltern memories, which contradicted the inaugural speech at the Museum, these two women activists not only reminded President Bachelet that her own administration did not fulfill the promise of social justice in Chile; they also made it clear that no institutional narrative of the memory of human rights violations could ever be imposed as a cohesive representational matrix that would take responsibility for the past if it only invoked the names of certain victims recognized by the state, while others remained ignored and unprotected by its laws. Catrileo and Vergara Toledo's protest reminds us that the struggles for identity and speech that emerge at all intersections of the map of power and resistance (which diagrams the relations between identity, community, and society) require the work of (a diversely striated, not smooth) memory that would be capable not only of engendering solidarity with the victims of the military dictatorship but also of taking a position in response to present antagonisms – like the Mapuche conflict – and of recognizing these oppressed and marginalized subjects as victims of a nonegalitarian democracy. The contingency of unpredictable protest movements that emerge at new points where the social fabric is torn, taking the shape of interruptions and disruptions, such as Catrileo and Vergara Toledo's intervention, destabilizes the hegemonic will to recuperate the past attempted by the Museum of Memory and Human Rights. The performativity of these women's intervention caused the ceremonial narrative of the Museum's inaugural celebration to come face to face with the turmoil and unrest generated by an off-script demand expressed by a rebellious memory: a memory that communicated an explosive sign to the discourse of reconciliation – namely, that it should always remain alert to the untimely emergence of unreconciled fragments that *also* demand their own justice.

The contortions of memory

During the Transition, the memory of the dictatorship revolved around one primary motif: the condemnation of the military regime's homicidal violence and the long-prohibited memory of its human rights violations, accompanied by demands for unfulfilled justice. From all their insistence and persistence, the victims' traumatic memory of the dictatorship managed to break through into a relative, democratic consensus that today strives to respect the slogan "Never again!" – even though among some sections of the Right, these efforts owe more to political opportunism than to ethical conviction. Does this relative (partial, unstable), democratic consensus about the need to condemn human rights violations mean that Chilean society has settled its accounts with memory? The answer is obviously no. The cultural and symbolic struggle between opposed versions of our memory remains just under the surface. This was demonstrated by the commemoration of the fortieth anniversary of the military coup, which was particularly eloquent in its ability to sharpen new debates about the recollection of the past, of history, and of memory. It would take a long time to enumerate the problems and dilemmas that were partially opened up by these new debates and which shook public discourse with unusual vigor. Some of the most obvious effects of this commemoration that also generated significant internal divisions along the Right include, for example: some right-wing officials, such as UDI senator Hernán Larraín, "asking for forgiveness" for the mistakes they made;[6] expanding the boundaries of the "military" to include the "civilian–military" segments of the dictatorship in order to ensure guilt would be assigned not just to the Armed Forces but also to the active and passive civilian accomplices of Pinochet's regime, such as the media and the judicial apparatus;[7] and CNN's interview with Manuel Contreras and President Piñera's surprising order to close Cordillera prison.[8] All of this happened on the occasion of the fortieth anniversary of the military coup, thanks to the public appearances of victims, witnesses, and participants whose primary and secondary accounts had been marginalized from the sphere of communication during the Transition – and thanks as well to the informational excess of a political present still reeling from the upheaval of the Matthei–Bachelet electoral campaign of 2013. This reflux of memory, which stirred social consciousness during the coup's fortieth anniversary, confirms the need to continue increasing the circulation and exchange of recollections about a disputed past that should be reevaluated at each new conjuncture of public debate. First, because the truth about the magnitude of the horror of the dictatorship – a truth that has been censored by multiple obfuscations – continues to be a truncated, incomplete truth, and every new piece of evidence of the dictatorship's crimes and abuses demonstrably reinforces the condemnations of the regime's opponents and critics. Second, because new pedagogies for the transmission of memory must be devised to revitalize the politics of remembrance, generating multiple displacements and translations between different writings that cross the narrated past (history) with the past narrating itself (memory) in a dialogical intersection with the memory of the present situation in action. This was demonstrated by the intensification of historical memory that, during the fortieth anniversary of the coup, pulsated with an unusual power of interpellation owing (undoubtedly!) to the repoliticization of society, which was activated by both the 2011 student movement and the imaginary of the YES versus NO plebiscite as a theater of antagonism that was projected onto the 2013 presidential elections in Chile.

From the sacrifice and defeat of Unidad Popular's interrupted project, mutilated by the coup, the moral and ethical dominion of the recollections of the vanquished was preserved during the long years of the Transition in a condensed memory around the body of the victim as an allegory for the violent crimes of torture and disappearance committed by the military, which tried to annihilate anything that was connected in solidarity to the figure of Salvador Allende (subjectivities, biographies, militancies, ideologies, and affects). The memory of those defeated and persecuted by the dictatorial regime, which was devoted to the victims identified as such by reports on human rights, with their emblematic recollections of torture and disappearance, perhaps prevents us from maintaining a timely awareness of the subterranean flows of another memory – that of the anonymous victims – that dwells within us every day. This would not be a condensed memory but, rather, a diluted one that branches out into habits and norms of obedience, into practical recommendations, into false commercial gratifications. This other, expanded memory, which has insidiously infiltrated our entire society, is the diluted and ramified memory of the legacy of the dictatorship which, through the Constitution of 1980, still governs us, treating all of us like objects of prejudice and attack, of offenses and privations, of economic mistreatment and sociopolitical disregard. This is all because of the structural violence of the civilian–military regroupment, which the dictatorship effectively used to combine the doctrine of neoliberalism ("social market economy") with the organic constitutionality of the authoritarian state (the Constitution of 1980). Thanks to the precedent set by the anti-neoliberal protests of the 2011 student movement, the commemoration of the fortieth anniversary of the military coup in 2013 managed to imprint the same accusatory mark on both memories: on the condensed memory of the victims who suffered repressive violence at the hands of the dictatorship in the past (a memory that rekindles indignation with the detailed resurgence of journalistic and audiovisual archives connected to the violation of human rights) and the anonymous memory, massively diluted in the present, of the continuity of the constitutional matrix designed by Jaime Guzmán, which advocates the extreme defense of private property, free enterprise, and capitalism and which, by the way, disallows any public form of collective self-organization. The commemoration of the fortieth anniversary of the coup made visible the double thread of condensed and diluted memory that connects the past of the dictatorship to the post-Transition present.

It is true that the memory of the coup completely invaded the sphere of televisual communications in September 2013, but what is also true is that the fleetingness of televised images gives the event (even events labeled as "historical recollections") an evanescent quality whose trace of memory disappears from the screen as quickly as it appears, almost without leaving any signs of its appeal. The screens where networks exchange their instantaneous flows never cease to saturate us with images, not even for a second. The operations of memory must recall that the slippage of audiovisual media ends up manufacturing oblivion by favoring the *circulation* of images over their *retention*. The erasability of memory that circulated through electronic media during the month of September 2013 was the first warning sign that we should be suspicious of the recollections of televised broadcasts of the coup's fortieth anniversary and their supposed ability to generate some lasting effect with regard to the recovery of historical memory. Consequently, after the intensive and extensive performativity of memory in September 2013, the commemoration of the coup's anniversary the following year in September 2014 (the first year of the Nueva Mayoría [New Majority] administration led by Michelle Bachelet) passed without any sort of fanfare, subsuming this acknowledgment of the past (a past that was a painful part of the collective biography of those who had voted as a majority for it) in the utter insignificance of an easily forgotten political present. This would be yet another form of proof that we are unable to shift the balance of memory that induces omissions, lapses, and intermittencies in what we remember.

There had already been a first lapse in the discourse of memory that was particularly shocking due to the circumstances surrounding it: the speech made from the balcony of La Moneda on March 11, 2010, which is to say, shortly after the massive earthquake of February 2010, by the newly elected President Sebastián Piñera, whose Alianza por Chile party had assumed power after four consecutive Concertación administrations. Completely changing the register of disappearance, which, through the politics of memory was associated with the sphere of human rights, Piñera appropriated and expropriated the category of "victim" that shook the foundations of the archive of memory by including in his speech the following surprising reference to those affected by the earthquake: "*We are going to keep looking for those who remain disappeared in the blue ocean that has not returned them.* " It was difficult for the families of those tortured and disappeared by the military regime to comprehend the image of Piñera celebrating his electoral triumph from the same balcony of the Palacio de la Moneda that was bombed in 1973 at the hands of political forces that were to be found among the supporters of his right-wing candidacy. However, even more unimaginable for the families of the victims of a regime characterized by its criminal expertise in disappearances was to listen to the Alianza por Chile's program for "change," which rhetorically inaugurated its coming to power by "changing" the core meaning of social memory. In effect, Piñera's speech removed the figure of the disappeared from the sphere of human rights, which has traditionally been mobilized by a Leftist sensibility (a memory that does not forget the bodies thrown into the ocean out of military aircraft during the dictatorship), to surreptitiously relocate this undeniably political figure to the domain of natural catastrophe. After so much effort and sacrifice during the Transition to inscribe in the public sphere the truth of disappearance as synonymous with an execrable past, the word "disappeared" was taken out of the commemorative universe that identified the military regime's victims by Piñera's astonishing discursive leap, with which he sought to diminish his well-known connections to the memory of the dictatorship. The president's speech effectuated an emptying of political content from memory which caused the category of victim to recover its passive innocence within a broad spectrum of natural disasters, while, in turn, the Alianza por Chile's agenda ably instrumentalized the earthquake to give political legitimacy to their (right-wing) efforts toward "national reconstruction." The transfer of the word "disappeared" from the realm of ethical and civic references to human rights to the deceptive context of a president's speech, in which he took advantage of the earthquake to justify his national speaking tour, marked a disturbing slippage of memory which demonstrated (among other things) that one cannot naively trust that the narrative of the past will remain definitively circumscribed by a vocabulary of names and characteristics whose significance is fixed for all time. The astonishing conjugation of disaster and misfortune that unsettlingly characterized

Chile between the earthquake of February 2010 and the beginning of Piñera's presidency – and the coming to power of a right-wing alliance – in March 2010 showed us that the historical memory of the dictatorship as tragedy (which was so costly to save from oblivion) would always be in danger of being overturned by the peculiarities and paradoxes of a present that shamelessly inverts the meanings of words that were once inextricably linked to the victims of state terrorism by de-emphasizing their criminal origins.

Again in 2015, one year into Bachelet's second administration, there was another slippage that in a new, unexpected turn shook the lexicon within which the language of memory is socially articulated. The word *truth* – connected to *justice* and *reparations* in the chain of discourse that condemns human rights violations – became less clear-cut by being combined with the word *falsity*, which began to appear prosaically on the front pages of national media outlets to refer to the "ideological falsity" of accounting documents that incriminated large corporations in tax evasion, as well as to condemn the enormous fiasco of the illegal financing of politicians by these same businesses during the Transition.[9] The demands to reveal what had been hidden (tirelessly led by groups of victims' families) had their subjects and objects changed, thus diverting the attention that had up to that point been focused on the dictatorship's crimes toward an emphasis on the secret arrangements made by the official bureaucracies of both supporters and opponents of the government during the Transition. This displacement of the lexicon (from crimes against humanity toward politics and business) made it so that talk even began to emerge of forming a "truth commission" (extrapolating from the historical significance of commissions focused on matters of human rights) to compel political leaders from both the Right and the Left to make their hidden relations with these corporations definitively transparent with regard to electoral contributions.[10] The word "falsity," which captured the attention of the media in 2013 and began to move from the realm of *ethics* (demanding truth and justice in cases of abduction, torture, and disappearance that were investigated and reported on by human rights commissions) to the *legal* sphere (transparency with regard to contributions that financed various political activities during the Transition), also perversely contaminated the debate over memory.[11] The word "falsity," which obscured everything with its cloak of doubts, obligated Chilean society to regretfully recognize that the political parties of the Left – the same parties that had struggled against the dictatorship and represented the victims of human rights violations – benefited from money donated by Pinochet's son-in-law and the principal looter of state enterprises during the dictatorship: Julio Ponce Lerou, CEO of SQM, who extended his wide-reaching networks of protection over the entire political class in order to guarantee impunity with regard to his fortune's exploitative origins, amassed under the protection of his ex-dictator father-in-law. The public revelation of these financial connections to Ponce Lerou marked the Left with the perfidious stigma of betrayal for having accepted political contributions from figures connected to the dictatorship that persecuted and disappeared thousands of victims who were politically on the Left.

Memory seems to have deviated from its course (that of the pursuit of the truth about the crimes of torture and disappearance) only to become lost among invoices and ballots, advisors and consultants, in the bureaucratic thickets of the networks of political power and influence that run throughout society as such, reflected every week in the "economics and business" sections, dedicated to the feverish activity of the markets, which fill almost all the pages of the national newspapers. After the commemoration of the fortieth anniversary of the military coup and the consequent explosion of historical memory in the media, these same newspapers forgot this memory once again and devoted themselves to news about the fiscal crimes of the Internal Tax Bureau and the economic decisions of the Public Prosecutor's office. However, in the middle of this situation, the contemporary political frame was struck by a new onslaught. Former conscript Fernando Guzmán finally revealed the truth about the "Quemados" ["Burn victims"] case, which occurred on July 2, 1986, when Carmen Gloria Quintana and Rodrigo Rojas de Negri were doused in gasoline and burned alive by a military patrol, thus breaking the "pact of silence" that the Armed Forces

had kept for twenty-nine years to cover up their responsibility for the crime. Beginning with the account related
by Guzmán and the testimony of Quintana, who survived
the attack, the present of the living, testifiable memory of
atrocities committed by the military dictatorship, the secret
machinations of the Armed Forces to cover up both the fate
of the bodies of the disappeared, and the identities of those
responsible for disappearing them in the first place returned
to the front pages. A final attack on memory, launched by
human rights and civil society organizations as a response to
Guzmán's testimony about the Quemados case, demanded
the demotion of the military personnel convicted of these
crimes that were still on active duty; the closure of the
Punta Pueco prison and the transfer of military convicts to
a high-security facility to put an end to any special status;
and the reform of the Military Code of Justice and the
breaking of the pacts of silence tacitly affirmed by both
civilians and military personnel to protect the Army. When
the memory of the dictatorship already appeared to have
once again dissipated in the sensational news of crimes of
political corruption, the truth revealed by Fernando Guzmán
reopened a public political evaluation of the behavior of
the Transition administrations with regard to human rights,
revealing their limitations and modifications, as well as their
methods of obstructing criminal evidence.

However, what is there in common between, on the one
hand, the legal pursuit of fiscal misconduct that shows the
financial corruption of the political parties of the Transition
through the "ideological falsity" of their accounting and,
on the other hand, the way in which this same Transition
relativized the ethical demand for absolute truth about the
abuses of the past by subordinating political management
of the truth to the hierarchy of military power committed
to the obstruction of justice? What both situations – the
tainted connections between the politics of the Transition
and its financial improprieties and the immoral obstruction
of justice of the secret pacts between military officials and
civilians under the formula of custodial justice – share is their
common origin: the Constitution of 1980 signed by Jaime
Guzmán as a legally binding document designed to protect
the political and economic privileges of those who inherited

both the dictatorship's legacy and its criminals.[12] Only if we revoke this Constitution for reasons of "ideological falsity" will the memory of the past – of both the dictatorship and the Transition – find itself in the realm of the future.

Notes

Introduction: The Struggle for Words

1   Acceptance speech of the Doctorate honoris causa, Universidad Central de las Villas (December 28, 1959). https://www.marxists. org/espanol/guevara/59-honor.htm (January 2018). Fidel Castro spoke to intellectuals using similar terms in his "Words to the Intellectuals" (1961).

2   You can read more about this controversy in Willy Thayer, "El Golpe como consumación de la vanguardia."

3   An expanded edition – which included reflections on Richard's book by the artists Norbert Lechner, Diamela Eltit, Pablo Oyarzún, Eugenio Dittborn, and others – was published in FLACSO in 1987.

4   I have opted for quotation marks because this process was not entirely democratic. In 1988, a plebiscite was held to determine whether General Pinochet should or should not remain in power: 55.9 percent of the population voted against his continued governance, and elections were called for the following year. In any case, the elections followed the norms of the military government, which in 1980 had modified the Constitution with transitory provisions that conditioned the democratic process.

Prologue

1 [The Concertación de Partidos de la Democracia (Coalition of Parties for Democracy) was a coalition of center-left political parties in Chile founded in 1988. This coalition won every presidential election from 1990 (when the dictatorship ended) until 2010. It was superseded in 2013 by the Nueva Mayoría (New Majority) party. —Tr.]

Chapter 1: Traces of Violence, Rhetoric of Consensus, and Subjective Dislocations

1 The numerous difficulties of investigating the mistrust between institutional, military, and present power structures are described in detail in various parts of Ascanio Cavallo's *La historia oculta de la transición*: "Patricio Aylwin assumes the presidency of the Republic on March 11, 1990, in a climate of acute tension between the new civil authorities and military commanders. Each of them is aware of their limitations and that they must carefully consider them ... How can one know the truth and do justice to violence committed in the past? Aylwin ruminates on this question, but he knows that he cannot avoid it. When he has a response, he must surmount formidable military opposition ... One group bears the heavy responsibility of preemptively removing the Army from political power: the Assessment Committee. Every operation of the first few months bears its marks ... The Minister of Justice, Francisco Cumplido, is in charge of the new government's two priority tasks: releasing political prisoners and achieving a balance in penal law. The grim evidence of the past emerges in opposition to these intentions" (11, 19, 29, 38).

2 "[A]ny objectivity is a threatened objectivity. If, in spite of this, an objectivity manages to partially affirm itself, it is only by repressing that which threatens it. To study the conditions of existence of a given social identity, then, is to study the power mechanisms making it possible." Laclau, *New Reflections on the Revolution of Our Time*, 31–32.

3 Moulian, *Chile actual*, 37, 39.

4 "These painless operations of the word" would today mark the precise zone where the catastrophic is consumed: "no longer in drama, in the disastrous world of what occurred politically but

rather in the debris of words, which today only inhabit symbolic rituals of vindication, repentance, and demonization, or of the ruins of what has already been said." Nicolás Casullo, "Una temporada en las palabras," 17.

5 "Devoid of the Great Project, the everyday turns into what is: the life of each and all days. Healthy minimalism? Maybe so. We all have our little projects, filling up the day, the week, the month, the year at most … missions which are disseminated by way of programs, initiatives that are born and die: local proposals … minimalism has been converted into a well-regarded value for daily action." Martín Hopenhayn, *No Apocalypse, No Integration*, 5, 8.

6 The AFDD remarked: "It is sad and a terrible mediocrity to renounce these *absolute* values for other *relative* ones." *Recuento de Actividades* 1992, 148.

7 Moreiras, "Postdictadura y reforma del pensamiento," 27.

8 Moreiras, "Postdictadura y reforma del pensamiento," 27.

9 "For many of the converts who have today made careers for themselves in some avenues of the system, forgetting represents the dark symptom of remorse over the life they denied. This forgetting is a means of protection from lacerating memories, perceived at times as nightmares, ghostly reminiscences of what has been lived. It is a forgetting interwoven with guilt. A shame, unnamed and unsayable, for infidelity toward others and toward one's own life, the shame of collusion and of coexistence." Moulian, *Chile actual*, 32.

10 Bravo, *4 ensayos y un poema*, 25.

11 Bravo, *4 ensayos y un poema*, 25.

12 Bravo, *4 ensayos y un poema*, 25.

Chapter 2: Women in the Streets: A War of Images

1 On September 21, 1998, Pinochet – occupying the role of Senator-for-Life, which had been secured for him in the Constitution of 1980 by military decree – traveled to London for spinal surgery. Without anyone suspecting, on October 10, 1998, Judge Baltasar Garzón of the Spanish Audiencia Nacional [National Court] issued an extradition order for Pinochet with the intention of interrogating him about the murder of Spanish citizens during the dictatorship in Chile, as well as with regard to crimes of genocide and torture. Pinochet was arrested and transferred to a clinic in London where he remained in police custody

for sixteen months. In England, a complex judicial process was initiated that ultimately determined that, due to his failing health, Pinochet was unable to stand trial. After being released on March 2, 2000, Pinochet was returned to Chile through the combined efforts of the British and Chilean governments. In Chile, Pinochet's case was dismissed due to his supposed mental health problems. Although several charges were subsequently brought against him, Pinochet died in December 2006 without ever being tried for his crimes.

2 It is worth consulting here the account of the "Women's War" that Sonia Montecino records in her analysis of the "maternal politics" mobilized by the Right as a counterrevolutionary force during the Unidad Popular era. See Montecino, *Madres y huachos*, 101–108.

3 In the letter, which was addressed to the President of the Republic Eduardo Frei Ruiz Tagle, and reproduced as an open letter in the national press, Pinochet wrote from London: "Beyond my pain and the wounds I bear in my soul from the unjust harassment to which I have been subjected, I want to express that I accept this new cross to bear with the humility of a Christian and the courage of a soldier … I pray that mine was the final sacrifice. I pray that my pain and the offenses of which I have been the victim may satisfy the infinitely insatiable thirst for vengeance." See Uribe and Vicuña, *El accidente Pinochet*, 165.

4 Bakhtin, *Rabelais and His World*, 153.

5 Needless to say, the cynicism of the Chilean Right's claim to national autonomy and sovereignty in response to Pinochet's arrest completely ignores the USA's multiple "interventions" (both economic and political) in Chile, which supported the Right in its anti-socialist battle against the Allende government.

Chapter 3: Torments and Obscenities

1 See Arce, *El infierno* and Merino, *Mi verdad*.

2 Hence, an article published about Arce's and Merino's books in the magazine *Hoy* was titled "Confesiones de seis agentes de la DINA: las mujeres no saben callar."

3 Merino, *Mi verdad*, 6.

4 Merino, *Mi verdad*, 8.

5 Contreras was appointed as the head of DINA by Augusto Pinochet, and in this role he directed a campaign of repressive activities (including kidnapping, torture, and murder) between

1973 and 1977. Before being sentenced to life in prison for multiple violations of human rights, he was first given in 1995 a sentence of seven years – for the murder of [opponent of the dictatorship] Orlando Letelier in Washington, DC. Refusing to go to prison, he voluntarily admitted himself to the Naval Hospital in Talcahuano, where he remained between June and October before finally being relocated to the penitentiary at Punta Pueco.

6 Arce, *El infierno*, 339.
7 Arce, *El infierno*, 339.
8 Arce asks: "And … am I not a woman? He gave me hundreds of explanations. I wasn't convinced, but in those days what was more important to me than anything was to be considered a militant." *El infierno*, 51.
9 Arce, *El infierno*, 56.
10 For an analysis of the meanings of torture and, in particular, of the relation between power, the body, and the voice, see Scarry, *The Body in Pain*.
11 Arce, *El infierno*, 78.
12 Arce, *El infierno*, 78 (emphasis added).

Chapter 4: Confessions of a Torturer and His (Abusive) Journalistic Assemblage

1 Nancy Guzmán is a Chilean journalist who lived in exile for several years in Colombia. Upon returning to Chile she expressed her commitment to human rights by publishing various investigative reports oriented around reconstructing the darkest past of the military dictatorship.
2 Romo was the Dirección de Inteligencia Nacional [National Intelligence Directorate] (DINA) agent in charge of repressing opponents of the military dictatorship between 1973 and 1977. Known as "Gautón [Fatso] Romo," he was one of the most infamous DINA torturers and one of the few who explicitly acknowledged his actions, which consisted primarily of the torture and sexual abuse of women detainees.
3 Guzmán, *Romo*, 17.
4 I agree with the ethical critique issued by the Latin American Institute of Mental Health and Human Rights in response to the book, which alleged that "when the resurgence of a traumatic experience is provoked without any respect for or solidarity with the victims, it produces an aggression that in a certain way repeats the repressive violence. Such cases are referred to as re-traumatization because the original trauma has wounded

the victims again, reproducing the abandonment and isolation of the first experience." See "Confesiones de Romo."

5 Arfuch, "Confesiones, conmemoraciones," 9.
6 Guzmán, *Romo*, 17 (italics added).
7 Guzmán, *Romo*, 22. [Adolfo Scilingo is a former Argentine naval officer who was convicted in 2005 of crimes against humanity for his role in the torture and extrajudicial execution of Leftists during the Dirty War in Argentina. He is currently serving a thirty-year sentence in a Spanish prison. –Tr.]
8 Guzmán, *Romo*, 182 (italics added).
9 Guzmán, *Romo*, 42, 14.
10 Guzmán, *Romo*, 218.
11 Guzmán, *Romo*, 42.
12 Guzmán, *Romo*, 41, 15.
13 Guzmán, *Romo* (italics added).
14 Guzmán, *Romo*, 25.
15 The Latin American Institute of Mental Health and Human Rights has stated: "In the book's lengthy reporting format, the interviewee seems to grow larger and gradually obscure the journalist, obliging the reader to endure his thuggish strutting and threats. At times, it is as if the torturer himself has taken possession of the book and begun to use it in part for his own ends ... The interviewer hardly ever confronts him ... Instead, she appears to orient, stimulate, and gently provoke this terrible individual to keep speaking and revealing ... The option she chose was to present the ex-torturer in the most intense way. It is like exhibiting a conflagration in order to demonstrate what a flame is like. It accomplishes the objective, but there is some risk of being burned again." "Confesiones de Romo," 24.
16 Guzmán, *Romo*, 144.
17 Guzmán, *Romo*, 175
18 Guzmán, *Romo*, 175.
19 Guzmán, *Romo*, 65, 107, 41, 65, 65, 174, 181.
20 Guzmán, *Romo*, 65, 67 (italics added).
21 Guzmán, *Romo*, 17 (italics added).
22 Guzmán, *Romo*, 17.
23 Guzmán, *Romo*, 65.
24 Guzmán, *Romo*, 165, 182 (italics added).
25 Guzmán, *Romo*, 208.
26 Guzmán, *Romo*, 223 (italics added).
27 Guzmán, *Romo*, 29.
28 Guzmán, *Romo*, 24.
29 Guzmán, *Romo*, 221, 27, 227.
30 Guzmán, *Romo*, 225.

Chapter 5: Coming and Going

1 Hernán Soto Henríquez, quoted in Aguirre and Chamoro, *"L"*: *Memoria gráfica del exilio chileno, 1973–1989*, 18.
2 Patricio Guzmán, quoted in Rufinelli, *Patricio Guzmán*, 282 (italics added).
3 Rufinelli, *Patricio Guzmán*, 282–283.
4 Guzmán states in an interview included in Rufinelli's book, "I think that *La batalla de Chile* is an unrepeatable film. I had the opportunity of finding myself in a unique situation, and I filmed it enthusiastically. That will never happen again." Quoted in Rufinelli, *Patricio Guzmán*, 340.
5 [La Moneda is the seat of the President of the Republic of Chile and was bombarded by the Chilean Air Force during the coup of September 11, 1973. –Tr.]
6 This is the off-screen text read by Guzmán over footage of the performance in *La memoria obstinada*.
7 Rufinelli, *Patricio Guzmán*, 289.
8 Castillo in Bedregal, "La dictadura convirtió a Chile en país de amnesia general" (italics added).
9 Castillo in Bedregal, "La dictadura convirtió a Chile en país de amnesia general" (italics added).
10 ["We, the *miristas* (militants of the MIR). –Tr.]
11 Echeverría and Castillo, *Santiago-París: El vuelo de la memoria*, 184–185.
12 Echeverría and Castillo, *Santiago-París*, 186.
13 As Castillo says: "Yes, much has been said about violence, but I don't know if that much has been said about militancy. I have spoken often with women ex-combatants from Chile, Argentina, and Uruguay about, for example, our relationship to guns. Is it a symbol of power, an extension of the phallus, or did we have our own way of possessing them and using them for something particular? Feminism obliges us to reflect on things like these." Quoted in Bedregal, "La dictadura convirtió a Chile en país de amnesia general."

Chapter 6: Architectures, Stagings, and Narratives of the Past

1 "In a personal interview conducted in January 2002, Mr. Pedro Matta, one of the principal activists who fought for the creation

of the Park for Peace, alluded to the political conflicts that
the park elicited, even among representatives of the political
Left. Matta said: 'I particularly remember a meeting with a
Socialist deputy who was very active in human rights matters.
Unexpectedly, and much to our surprise, he told us that he would
not support the construction of a Park for Peace because he
believed that Chile's fledgling democracy and its recently established institutions could not handle it. He thought there might
be a reaction from the army that could endanger the status quo
or undermine the agreements and understandings that had been
reached to establish "governability" in the country. Because
of this, he was willing to support the construction of a human
rights park anywhere but at Villa Grimaldi.'" Lazzara, *Chile in
Transition: The Poetics and Politics of Memory*, 197.

2 For a detailed history of Patio 29, see Bustamante and Ruderer,
Patio 29.

3 Derrida, *Specters of Marx*, 9 (italics in original).

4 Bustamante and Ruderer, *Patio 29*, 109 (italics added).

5 From a document included in the project *Un espacio de
Memoria en Construcción* [The Construction of a Space of
Memory], produced by the Londres 38 Workshop, Casa de la
Memoria, 2008.

6 The project *Un espacio de memoria en construcción* tells us that
it "proposes to preserve the building as the place of privileged
memory insofar as it is a former clandestine repression and
torture facility run by the principal repressive state apparatus
(DINA), the Yucatán Detention Center. This implies a museo-
graphic concept that considers the house to be the only [*único*]
object in a collection – unique [*único*] because in principle there
were no other objects to put in a collection, but it is also unique
[*único*] because the house itself is irreplaceable as a symbol of
the Detention Center." www.londres38.cl.

7 Vinyes, "Sobre Londres 38."

8 Vinyes, "Sobre Londres 38."

9 The counterpoint of shadow posited by Alfredo Jaar's work
La geometría de conciencia [The Geometry of Conscience] to
this luminosity and transparency of the Museum of Memory
is interesting in the way that it is (inversely) constructed like a
crypt: an installation located on one side of the museum in a
basement level which submerges the visitor into the enigmatic
obscurity of a room prepared specifically to communicate the
sensation of imprisonment and thus to make this confinement
such a disturbing experience that visitors will feel unsettled by
the mystery of what awaits them in the darkness below. The

quietness of the room, as well as its protocols of entry, which imbue it with a sense of ritual and initiation, evoke a worshipful quality of memory that distinguishes this exhibit from the rest of the Museum.

10 Benjamin, "Experience and Poverty," 733–734.

11 In charge of the Museum of Memory and Human Rights' mueseographic staging and interior architecture is Árbol de Color, a firm "that combines and complements design and marketing to contribute to the strategic and creative development of a brand, product, or service ... creating communicational solutions through architecture, design, art, marketing, and entertainment." www.arbolcolor.cl.

Chapter 7: Two Stagings of the Memory of YES and NO

1 "The [anti-dictatorship] opposition's dilemma ... was either to remain voluntarily marginalized from the new scenario and its institutionality or to accept it and act within it ... The nearly unanimous opinion in the early 1980s, after the regime had imposed its Constitution, was that opposition to Pinochet was at a turning point. The established paths began to diverge. While some of us set about burying 'the resistance' with honor and constructing a subject capable of acting in the 'new scenario,' on the Left, precisely the opposite thesis began to gain force: what had actually led to failure was *peaceful* resistance." Tironi, *Sin miedo, sin odio, sin violencia*, 80.

2 Larraín is a young Chilean filmmaker who has attained both recognition and success with films like *Tony Manero* (2008), *Post Mortem* (2019), *No* (2012), and *El Club* (2015).

3 Tironi, *Sin miedo, sin odio*, 268.

4 "Larraín ... works from the point of view of someone who is disconnected from his environment, preoccupied by bringing home the bacon and just wanting to do 'a good job' – the opposite of an epic hero. It is a de-dramatized and distanced point of view ... However, in turn, *No* is a film that is symptomatic of contemporary politics. Its visualization of the 'political emptying out' at the hands of the 'market' ... opens up a gap in the origin of democracy that we might call the Concertación government's 'originary betrayal' of social movements. It also responds to the origins of Tironi et al.'s think-tanks, media monopolies, and the world of advertising as a configuration of social imaginaries. Like it or not, the film relates the point of

view of this 'social subject,' whose role is that through which images, signs, and media construct collective imaginaries ... Larraín has understood the value of the 'rise' of the melancholic commodity, the postmodern consumption of pastiche." Pinto, "*No*, de Pablo Larraín."

5 Moulian, *Chile actual*, 145.

6 Larraín remarks: "In *No* there is a dialogue where Antonia (Zegers)'s character says to Gael (García Bernal)'s character: 'Man, voting in this plebiscite is saying "yes" to Pinochet's Constitution.' She says to vote in the plebiscite is to endorse the dictatorship. And this has something premonitory about it in the sense that the people who opposed the plebiscite, who were not so few in number, realized that they were negotiating and that this could have negative consequences in the future. It was important to me to address this in the movie: how to negotiate and represent a model that has now been abused in the present.... This pact, this social logic was formed in the plebiscite." "Entendiendo a Pablo Larraín."

7 Foster, *The Return of the Real*, 10 (italics added).

8 Rancière, *The Emancipated Spectator*, 14.

9 "The movie was filmed with the U-matic ¾-inch video equipment commonly used at the end of the 80s, which makes it so the texture and color of Chilean television from that era blend well with the fictional scenes ... *To use film stock or contemporary high definition digital cameras would have generated a distance from the images of the era. This blending was important, and now that I've seen the final cut I can't really tell which is the footage we shot and which is from television.*" Larraín, quoted in "Película chilena sobre el plebiscite de 1988 es aclamada en Cannes" (italics added).

10 Tironi, *Los silencios de la revolución*, 302.

11 Tironi maintains that "Chileans ... aspired to social mobility and economic progress; in this regard, they were not disgusted by the 'economic model' imposed by Pinochet. In other words, they wanted to gain access to the process of modernization in the country that was talked about so much and that was already noticeable in different areas, particularly on the level of consumption." *Los silencios de la revolución*, 198.

12 Lavín, *Chile: revolución silenciosa*, 151.

13 "The Mexican star of *No*, Gael García, came to our country in order to engage in different promotional activities for Larraín's film. It was in this capacity that the actor met with Camila Vallejo and Giorgio Jackson, as well as other student leaders, to view the film last Sunday. The Mexican actor also expressed

his appreciation for the student movement. García Bernal remarked that Confech (Confederación de Estudiantes de Chile [Confederation of Chilean Students]) is 'the most important movement on the planet. No other country has the election of its university coalitions on front pages around the world.' He additionally said, 'If I could dedicate this film to anyone it would be to you, the student movement'" (biobio.cl, July 30, 2012).

14 "Pablo Larraín – Cannes: Película 'NO' es una historia que 'merecía contarse.'"

15 Virno, *Déjà Vu and the End of History*, 8.

16 "The principal meaning of political action is always constituted from the perspective of the future anterior: in order to understand what we are doing today we must examine things from the perspective of the future, we must ask ourselves how it will look when in the future we remember the present moment as past. Another mode of expressing this same idea is to say that attributing political meaning to something is to insert it into a narrative ... The meaning of political action is in neither the past nor the future, but rather in the connection between the past and the future ... We need to know if what the Concertación governments did in those twenty years can be understood as part of the history of the triumph of neoliberalism in Chile or as part of the (pre-)history of Chilean socialism. We are less interested in knowing what happened during those twenty years than in what narrative has been recorded about the period ... We need to know if those twenty years will lead to a radically neoliberal future or a socialist one." Atria, *Veinte años después*, 12–16.

17 Although it could be merely anecdotal, there is something symptomatic about the way in which, within the film itself, Larraín inverts certain roles and characters, with Chilean actors who during the Transition were publicly affiliated with the NO campaign portraying individuals from the dictatorship who ran the YES campaign. It is almost as if this interchangeability of the sites of enunciation were yet another post-political game.

18 Piñera stated in an interview with the newspaper *La Tercera* on August 31, 2013: "Nearly the entire center-right of that era was in favor of YES. I often argued against this because I felt it was a profound mistake. To extend the military period by another eight years would have been to fail to understand that the country was ready for the recuperation of democracy and needed it like we need the air we breathe. But we all had the right to disagree. It doesn't matter to me if people make

mistakes; what worries me is when, afterward, with the benefit of more information and time to think about it, they insist on committing the same errors." http://www.latercera.com/noticia/presidente-sebastian-pinera-y-su-juicio-a-40-anos-del-golpe-hubo-muchos-que-fueron-complices-pasivos-que-sabian-y-no-hicieron-nada-o-no-quisieron-saber/.

19 Tironi, *Los silencios de la revolución*, 222.

20 [The Unión Democrática Independiente (Independent Democratic Union) is a right-wing party founded in Chile in 1983 by Jaime Guzmán, a conservative politician and law professor who was a close civilian advisor to Pinochet and one of the architects of the dictatorship's 1980 Constitution. –Tr.]

21 Novoa, *Con la fuerza de la libertad*, 168–170.

22 "Bachelet and Matthei confront one another, not as destined by their gender or as the fruit of their individual histories, but rather as the result of the projects they represent: one, Bachelet, is associated with an attempt to modify capitalist modernization as radically as possible; the other, Matthei, stands for the dying efforts to maintain that same capitalist modernization. One, Bachelet, represents the attempt to alter the lines of modernization that Chile began to follow in the 1980s, during the dictatorship; the other, Matthei, represents the effort to reinforce these same lines and make sure they are not erased or made more tenuous. One, Bachelet, is aligned with the demands of social movements; the other, Matthei, embraces the opposite of these demands." Peña, "¿Bachelet versus Matthei?"

23 Mouffe writes: "Another thesis concerns the nature of collective identities which always entail a we/they discrimination. They play a central part in politics and the task of democratic politics is not to overcome them through consensus but to construct them in a way that energizes the democratic confrontation ... To be able to mobilize passions towards democratic designs, democratic politics must have a partisan character. This is indeed the function of the left/right distinction ... Mobilization requires politicization, but politicization cannot exist without the production of a conflictual representation of the world, with opposed camps with which people can identify, thereby allowing for passions to be mobilized politically within the spectrum of the democratic process ... Consensus is needed on the institutions constitutive of democracy and on the 'ethico-political' values informing the political association – liberty and equality for all – but there will always be disagreement concerning their meaning and the way they should be implemented ... [D]emocracy requires a 'conflictual consensus': consensus on the ethico-political values

of liberty and equality for all, dissent about their interpretation."
On the Political, 5–6, 24–25, 31, 121.
24 Mouffe, *On the Political*, 17.

Chapter 8: Past–Present: Symbolic Displacements of the Figure of the Victim

1 This intervention was titled *¿Dónde están? ¿Dónde está? Intervención urbana: El caso de José Huenante* [Where are They? Where is He? Urban Intervention: The Case of José Huenante]. The artists who participated were Eugenio Téllez, Guillermo Núñez, Voluspa Jarpa, Carlos Montes de Oca, Ismael Frigerio, Víctor Pavez, Bernardo Oyarzún, Roser Bru, Iván Navarro, and Camilo Yáñez.
2 The Londres 38 Collective describes the urban intervention in the following way in the work's catalog: "The resulting images (of the artists' work), enlarged, occupy a dozen buildings along the Alameda in an attempt to appropriate the public space that other young people occupied in the past and which is today being recuperated for all by a new generation."
3 *Londres 38* catalog, 7.
4 Correa Bluas filed a Criminal Complaint before the Puerto Montt District Court on March 25, 2009 against those responsible for the abduction and disappearance of José Huenante. The failure to obtain any results in this case is connected to the fact that it was being handled by the Military Justice department, which has made it difficult to prosecute the three accused police officers.
5 *Londres 38* catalog, 57.
6 Butler, *Frames of War*, 38.
7 The Military Justice department has rejected all petitions to put the three police agents responsible for Huenante's abduction and disappearance on trial.
8 Yáñez remarks: "All of Chile demands to know where they are." He also says that the social critique in his work "attempts to show the front page of Chile's leading newspaper discussing the disappeared, even if only in a symbolic way, even if it is only for a day," since "if it is presented as a headline, people will be motivated to ask why such headlines don't actually appear in the newspapers." "Aunque se por un día," *Londres 38* catalog, 13.
9 Agustín Edwards Eastman, businessman and journalist, is a member of one of the oldest and most influential economic circles in Chile. He is the owner of *El Mercurio* and nineteen

other regional daily newspapers. He has been accused of receiving significant financial support from the CIA – he is named in the Church Report and in the CIA's own declassified documents – for efforts to destabilize the Unidad Poplar government. During the military dictatorship, he imposed an editorial line that silenced any mention of the Pinochet government's crimes against human rights and consequently became a powerful accomplice to the regime in exchange for favors that enriched his businesses. In 2014, the Association of Journalists – of which Edwards had been a member without ever being held responsible for any of the offenses he committed – decided to expel him for violating the organization's code of journalistic ethics with his repeated maneuverings to undermine democracy. Eliodoro Matte Larraín is the head of the third most powerful business organization in Chile, which, according to *Forbes* magazine, constitutes one of the largest fortunes in the world. He worked as an advisor to the Pinochet dictatorship's National Health Service before taking control over the holdings of the Matte group, which consolidated as the Paper and Cardboard Manufacturing Company (Empresas CMPC) within the logging industry. The 2010 reopening of a case about the September 1973 disappearance of nineteen citizens of Laja and San Rosendo, two towns in the region where *la Papelera* had been operating at the time, provided evidence that the company facilitated the development of lists of workers to be abducted and killed. See Javier Rebolledo, *A la sombra de los cuervos*.

10 As Rebolledo remarks, "According to its own communications, *El Mercurio* was one of the primary allies of *la Papelera* ... At all of its newsstands it promoted the campaign 'La Papelera ¡No!' ['Hands off *la Papelera*!'], a message which directly argued that the expropriation of Empresas CMPC (which held a monopoly on the paper used by Chilean periodicals) was a violation of the fundamental right to free expression." Rebolledo, *A la sombra de los cuervos*, 35.

Chapter 9: Media Explosion of Memory in September 2013

1 Stern, *Memorias en construcción*, 49.
2 Mónica Szurmuk provides the following definition of the term: "The term 'postmemory' originates within the field of memory studies in the United States toward the end of the 1980s to account for the experience of the generation of the children of

Holocaust survivors, but it has already been used to explain the perdurability of trauma in other contexts ... the term 'memory' is used to refer to the experience and the ensuing cultural production by its victims, witnesses, or perpetrators, while 'postmemory' focuses on the cultural registers produced by those who grew up in the shadow of those memories." *Dictionary of Latin American Cultural Studies*, 258–260.

3 *11 íntimo* described Martínez's experience in the following way: "Manuel Martínez is 32 years old and has been a cameraman for Televisión Nacional for five years. Along with other journalists that morning, he moved around from place to place trying to capture the tense but calm atmosphere. Suddenly, he noticed something that almost no one else did. At that moment, Martínez had no idea that he was filming the last moving images of Salvador Allende to ever be recorded."

4 *11 íntimo*, September 2013.

5 *11 íntimo*, September 2013.

6 Didi-Huberman, *Images in Spite of All*, 39.

7 Sontag, *Regarding the Pain of Others*, 21.

8 Groys, *Art Power*, 85.

9 Didi-Huberman et al., *Cuando las imágenes tocan lo real*, 15.

10 Taylor, *The Archive and the Repertoire*, 244.

11 Didi-Huberman et al., *Cuando las imágenes tocan lo real*, 41.

12 Sontag, *Regarding the Pain of Others*, 21.

13 *El año que cambió nuestras vidas*, September 2013.

14 *La voz de los 40*, September 2013.

15 "TVN a 40 años del golpe," *El Dínamo*, August 22, 2013.

16 *El Mercurio*, December 22, 2013.

17 Bañados, *Confidencias de un locutor*, 225.

18 Honorato is a journalist who, during the military dictatorship, worked for Canal 13 and other media organizations whose news broadcasts distorted facts and covered them up with false information provided by the dictatorship's communications apparatus. He has been accused by various human rights organizations of having collaborated, as a journalist, with the military regime. Up to this day, he continues to work in the same position, broadcasting his reports "from the Courts of Justice in Santiago."

19 Feliciano Cerda, an interviewee on the program *Mentiras verdaderas* on the Red network, August 28, 2013.

20 This prison and torture center (also known as the Tejas Verdes Regimentary School for Military Engineers, located in San Antonio province) was where, starting on September 11, 1973, systematic torture took place under the direction of DINA chief Manuel Contreras. See Rebolledo, *A la sombra de los cuervos*.

21 Olga Letellier, on the program *Mentiras verdaderas*, September 10, 2013.
22 González Rodríguez, "'Mamo' Contreras y la TV."
23 These were some of the statements Contreras made during the interview conducted by Matamala and Rincón, which was broadcast on CNN in unedited form on September 10, 2013.
24 "A heated and intense debate was generated yesterday in the political committee meeting at La Moneda, following the decision of President Sebastián Piñera to close the Cordillera Prison and transfer nine prisoners to the Punta Pueco detention center. The directorates of both the RN and the UDI directly told the ministers not to support the measure, going so far as to call it 'inopportune' ... In private, officials said that the decision to close the prison would be detrimental to Evelyn Matthei's candidacy. Some even estimated that the Alianza would lose votes not only from retired military and their families but also from civilians who make a distinction between Manuel Contreras and the deceased Odlanier Mena." Bentancourt, *Diario Financiero online*, October 1, 2013.

Chapter 10: Commemoration of the 40th Anniversary of the Military Coup ... and Afterwards

1 See Joignant, "El funeral de Pinochet," particularly the section "Un extraño tribunal."
2 See Rebolledo, *A la sombra de los cuervos.*
3 In a letter to *El Mercurio* on June 22, 2012, Villalobos writes of the Museum of Memory and Human Rights: "From the point of view of history, the museum's existence represents a desire to falsify the past, as it focuses on a singular event, separated from the rest of our history and therefore incomprehensible. The past must be understood in its totality, beginning with the particular history of each situation ... Missing from the aforementioned 'museum' is the background of the country's political and social situation. Missing in particular is the destruction of public ethics and the abuses, lies, and outrages of the Unidad Popular administration. It is not a matter of hiding official excesses but rather of seeking the explanation for why they occurred. Political individuals and movements always try to manipulate history and remember only what is convenient. But history is a science with rigorous methods that seek the entire truth, whatever it

may be. It is clear that the aforementioned 'museum' is part of the propaganda produced by political groups that, in response to the failure of their current activities, seeks out images and concepts that affirm the weakness of which they complain. I suggest reformulating its content and name: the Museum of the Failure of Unidad Popular and the Present."

4 The following letter, signed by the members of the Museum's board of directors (including María Luisa Sepúlveda, María Eugenia Rojas, Arturo Fontaine, Gastón Gómez, Milan Ivelic, Fernando Montes, Claudio Nash, Enrique Palet, Carlos Peña, Daniel Platovsky, Margarita Romero, Marcia Scantlebury Agustín Squella, and Carolina Tohá), was published in *El Mercurio* on June 30, 2012: "Dear Editor: Recently, there has been debate around the task of the Museum of Memory and Human Rights. This debate is good for public culture. However, there have been some misunderstandings about the task of the Museum (the board of which we are members of) that oblige us to state the following: 1. The task of the Museum of Memory and Human Rights is to promote a public awareness of the massive, systematic, and prolonged violation of those rights between September 11, 1973 and March 11, 1990, which is the period covered by the investigations of the Truth and Reconciliation Commission, published as the Rettig Report. 2. The purpose of this awareness promoted by the Museum has not a political but rather a moral purpose: to transform respect for human rights into a categorical imperative of coexistence – that is, as a duty for all that cannot be attenuated or diminished by any circumstance. 3. The Museum's task is therefore neither historiographical nor legal. Its purpose is not to provide information about the causes that led to these violations or that would contextualize them, nor to formulate accusations of individual responsibility, but to promote the idea that, regardless of the circumstances, such events should never again occur in our country. 4. The Museum is confident that its activities and exhibitions – which in the public interest must rely on state support – will challenge the public and thus promote considered debate and dialogue about respect for human rights. Finally, we invite all our fellow Chileans to visit the Museum and form their own opinions as to whether it fulfills the task for which it was created."

5 On January 3, 2008, Matías Catrileo was shot in the back and died at the Santa Margarita farm, located in the rural Vilcún area, which is part of ancestral Mapuche lands. A military tribunal imposed a two-year suspended sentence on Walter

Ramírez Inostroza, a lance corporal in the Carabineros who was the only person implicated in Catrileo's murder, even though José Pinto Aparicio, the military prosecutor of the Cautín province, had accused Ramírez Inostroza of unnecessary violence and requested a ten-year sentence. In the context of the victimization of the Mapuche community, Catrileo's murder and the ensuing trial serve as a symbol of the indifference and impunity that characterizes efforts to seek justice for these crimes.

6 In an article in *El Mercurio* from September 2, 2013, Larraín stated: "I am convinced that we are all responsible to some degree. Some through action, others through omission. Some by keeping quiet and others by remaining content with the official explanations. The return to democracy favored initiatives designed to clarify what happened, to seek truth and justice, to give symbolic and real recognition, to repair in some part the damage that had been done. Democracy and human rights are on the rise, but opinions about us haven't changed, especially for the victims or their families ... Will things always be this way for us? Is it possible to contribute to the reconciliation of our hearts? Is it possible to recognize our mistakes and to admit them to others? Can we conceive of a common path toward the construction of a peaceful and united country? ... So, I thought that asking for forgiveness was the path toward a healthy future for society. Whether one feels a lot or a little responsibility, every bit helps."

7 "There was undoubtedly a profound darkness about the military government, such as the repeated, permanent, and systematic abuse of human rights by agents of the state, or the loss of freedoms and the suppression of inalienable rights. But there was also light, such as the modernization of our society, economy, and institutions, opening up to the rest of the world, the implementation of the social market economy, and opportunities for individual initiative. All of this was positive and ahead of its time. But if we want to look for those responsible during the military government, especially with regard to abuses of human rights and personal dignity, there are of course many to be found – at the very least the highest authorities of the military government who knew or should have known what was happening. But it was not only them. There were also many passive accomplices – many who knew and did nothing or who didn't want to know and likewise did nothing. There were also judges who allowed themselves to be influenced and who denied resources or protection that would have saved many lives. There

were also journalists with front-page stories who knew what they had published did not correspond to the truth." Interview with Sebastián Piñera in *La Tercera*, August 31, 2013.

8 "The personal agenda unfurled by President Sebastian Piñera during the month of September, the fortieth anniversary of the military coup, took on a final flourish this afternoon with the announcement of the closure of the Cordillera Prison, where ten ex-military officers – led by ex-DINA chief Manuel Contreras – are serving sentences for crimes against humanity … This is the right-wing Piñera, without any baggage of any kind connected to the dictatorship, who in the last two decades has been involved in strengthening the liberal wing. In any case, the right answer will come at a cost. The government and its official political supporters warn that there will be conflicts with this other Right, which remains separate from September's presidential performance, that of the UDI and segments of RN, which, in the weeks leading up to the fortieth anniversary commemoration, protested several times at La Moneda against the tenor of Piñera's statements on this subject." "Piñera Cierra el Penal Cordillera," *El Mostrador*, September 26, 2013.

9 The first case to become known publicly in 2013 was that of the Penta Group, which was accused of massive fraud by the Chilean Treasury for allowing the irregular financing of various electoral campaigns connected to presidential candidates run by the Unión Democrática Independiente (UDI) party. Later, in 2015, public attention was focused on the case of the Sociedad Química y Minera de Chile (SQM; Chemical and Mining Society of Chile), which was privatized by the dictatorship and has been administered since then by Pinochet's ex-son-in-law, Julio Ponce Lerou. Investigations, which are still ongoing, demonstrated that the millions extracted from the silver mines had indirectly served to finance electoral campaigns by parties ranging from the UDI to the Socialist Party, involving, in addition to the political Right, leaders of the Concertación and the Nueva Mayoría.

10 "On his morning program on Radio Cero, the writer and first cousin of Marcos Enríquez Ominami, Rafael Gumucio, announced the idea of creating a commission to compel politicians to disclose their relations with businesses. 'There should be a "Truth Commission" formed to tell everyone that this is how politics was, this was how it worked, to tell everyone that we have it wrong and that we are going to change the system,' the writer commented, offering as an example a model similar to that developed in South Africa to overcome their period of

racial discrimination. Mandela did not become innocent with the system of apartheid, which was fundamentally evil and which has even blemished others. In Chile we have lived in an institutional political system that is fundamentally evil and which has even tainted irreproachable figures like President Bachelet." "Propuesta de Rafael Gumucio."

11 "The story of illegal political financing associated with SQM has spread out like an oil spill ... It is not surprising that Pinochet's son-in-law would have decided to fund right-wing political groups. What is significant, however, is that even some victims of the dictatorship have been open to receiving resources from him; that he could become a donor to General Bachelet's daughter's presidential campaign, or to the son of Miguel Enríquez, or that former minister Enrique Correa would be one of his main communications advisors. This has in some way exposed the degree of ethical corruption to which the political system has been taken by the current generation, and this profound, existential problem unfortunately has not yielded any legislation that would reform campaign financing." Colodro, "Padre nuestro."

12 Guzmán, the primary ideologue of the 1980 Constitution, defines the political framework of his perverse design in the following way: "Instead of governing to do, to a greater or lesser extent, what one's adversaries want, it is preferable to create a reality that obliges all who govern to submit to the demands of that reality. That is, if one's adversaries come to power, they will be restricted to following a course of action that is not so different from what one would desire anyway because the margin of alternatives that the field imposes on those who play on it would be sufficiently restricted so as to make any other option extremely difficult." "El camino politico," 19.

Bibliography

Aguirre, Estela and Sonia Chamoro. *"L"*: *Memoria gráfica del exilio chileno, 1973–1989*. Santiago: Ocholibros Editores, 2008.

Arce, Luz. *El infierno*. Santiago: Planeta, 1993.

Arfuch, Leonor. "Confesiones, conmemoraciones." *Punto de vista* 52 (August 1995): 6–11.

Atria, Fernando. *Veinte años después: Neoliberalismo con rostro humano*. Santiago: Catalonia, 2013.

Bakhtin Mikhail. *Rabelais and His World*. Trans. Hélène Iswolsky. Bloomington: Indiana University Press, 1984.

Bañados, Patricio. *Confidencias de un locutor*. Santiago: Cuarto Propio, 2013.

Bedregal, Ximena. "La dictadura convirtió a Chile en país de amnesia general." *La Jornada* (February 23, 2007).

Benjamin, Walter. "Experience and Poverty." In *Selected Writings, Volume 2: 1927–1934*. Cambridge, MA: Belknap/Harvard University Press, 1999, pp. 731–736.

Bravo, Germán. *4 ensayos y un poema*. Santiago de Chile: Intemperie Ediciones, 1996.

Bustamante, Javiera and Stephan Ruderer. *Patio 29: Tras la cruz de fierro*. Santiago: Ocho Libro Editores, 2009.

Butler, Judith. *Frames of War: When is Life Grievable?* London: Verso, 2009.

Casullo, Nicolás. "Una temporada en las palabras." *Confines* 3 (1996): 13–32.

Cavallo, Ascanio. *La historia oculta de la transición: Memoria de una época: 1990–1998*. Santiago de Chile: Grijalbo, 1998.

Colodro, Max. "Padre nuestro." *La Tercera* (February 7, 2016). http://www.latercera.com/voces/padre-nuestro/.

"Confesiones de Romo: ¿locura del verdugo o locura de la sociedad?" *Rocinante* 29 (March 2, 2001): 24.

Derrida, Jacques. *Specters of Marx: The State of the Debt, the Work of Mourning, and the New International.* Trans. Peggy Kamuf. London: Routledge, 1994.

Didi-Huberman, Georges. *Images in Spite of All: Four Photographs from Auschwitz.* Trans. Shane B. Lillis. Chicago: University of Chicago Press, 2008.

Didi-Huberman, Georges, Clément Chéroux, and Javier Arnaldo. *Cuando las imágenes tocan lo real.* Madrid: Círculo de Bellas Artes Madrid, 2013.

Echeverría, Mónica, and Carmen Castillo. *Santiago-Paris: El vuelo de la memoria.* Santiago: LOM Ediciones, 2002.

"Entendiendo a Pablo Larraín." *La Tercera*, Santiago (January 20, 2013).

Foster, Hal. *The Return of the Real: The Avant-Garde at the End of the Century.* Cambridge, MA: MIT Press, 1996.

González Rodríguez, Gustavo. "'Mamo' Contreras y la TV: escribir derecho con líneas torcidas." CIPER Chile (October 10, 2013). http://ciperchile.cl/2013/10/10/%E2%80%9Cmamo%E2%80%9D-contreras-y-la-tv-escribir-derecho-con-lineas-torcidas/.

Groys, Boris. *Art Power.* Cambridge, MA: MIT Press, 2008.

Guzmán, Jaime. "El camino politico." *Revista Realidad* 1:7 (1979): 13–23.

Guzmán, Nancy. *Romo: confesiones de un torturador.* Santiago de Chile: Editorial Planeta, 2001.

Hopenhayn, Martín. *No Apocalypse, No Integration: Modernism and Postmodernism in Latin America.* Trans. Cynthia Margarita Tompkins and Elizabeth Rosa Horan. Durham, NC: Duke University Press, 2001.

Joignant, Alfredo. "El funeral de Pinochet: Memoria, historia e inmortalidad." In Alfredo Joignant, Cath Collins, and Katherine Hite, eds. *Las políticas de la memoria en Chile: Desde Pinochet hasta Bachelet.* Santiago: Ediciones Universidad Diego Portales, 2013, pp. 193–226.

Laclau, Ernesto. *New Reflections on the Revolution of Our Time.* New York: Verso, 1990.

Lavín, Joaquín. *Chile: revolución silenciosa.* Santiago: Zig-Zag, 1987.

Lazzara, Michael. *Chile in Transition: The Poetics and Politics of Memory.* Gainesville: University of Florida Press, 2006.

Merino, Marcia Alejandra. *Mi verdad.* Santiago: AGT, 1994.

Montecino, Sonia. *Madres y huachos: alegorías del mestizaje chileno*. Santiago: Cuarto Propio, 1991.

Moreiras, Alberto. "Postdictadura y reforma del pensamiento." *Revista de Crítica Cultural* 7 (1993): 26–35.

Mouffe, Chantal. *On the Political*. Abingdon: Routledge, 2005.

Moulian, Tomás. *Chile actual: Anatomía de un mito*. Santiago: Arcis/Lom, 1997.

Novoa, Jovino. *Con la fuerza de la libertad: La batalla por las ideas de centro-derecha en el Chile de hoy*. Santiago: Planeta/La Tercera, 2012.

"Pablo Larraín – Cannes: Película 'NO' es una historia que 'merecía contarse.'" *La Nación* (May 26, 2012). www.lanacion.cl.

"Película chilena sobre el plebiscito de 1988 es aclamada en Cannes." *La Tercera* (May 26, 2012). www.latercera.com.

Peña Carlos. "¿Bachelet versus Matthei?" *El Mercurio* (August 4, 2013).

"Piñera cierra el Penal Cordillera y pone broche de oro a su agenda personal por los 40 años del golpe." *El Mostrador* (September 26, 2013).

Pinto, Iván. "*No*, de Pablo Larraín. En torno a recepciones y nominación …" http://elagentecine.cl/2013/01/10/no-de-pablo-larrain-en-torno-a-recepciones-y-nominacion/.

"Propuesta de Rafael Gumucio: 'Comisión Verdad" para crisis política." *La Segunda* (June 30, 2015).

Rancière, Jacques. *The Emancipated Spectator*. Trans. Gregory Elliot. London: Verso, 2009.

Rebolledo, Javier. *A la sombra de los cuervos: Los cómplices civiles de la dictadura*. Santiago: Ceibo, 2015.

Rufinelli, Jorge. *Patricio Guzmán*. Madrid: Cátedra, 2001.

Scarry, Elaine. *The Body in Pain: The Making and Unmaking of the World*. New York: Oxford University Press, 1985.

Sontag, Susan. *Regarding the Pain of Others*. New York: Farrar, Strauss and Giroux, 2003.

Stern, Steve J. *Memorias en construcción: los retos del pasado presente en Chile, 1989–2011*. Santiago: Museo de la Memoria y los Derechos Humanos, 2013.

Szurmuk, Mónica and Robert McKee Irwin, eds. *Dictionary of Latin American Cultural Studies*. Gainesville: University Press of Florida, 2012.

Taylor, Diana. *The Archive and the Repertoire: Performing Cultural Memory in the Americas*. Durham, NC: Duke University Press, 2003.

Tironi, Eugenio. *Los silencios de la revolución: Chile: la otra cara de la modernización*. Santiago: Editorial La Puerta Abierta, 1988.

Tironi, Eugenio. *Sin miedo, sin odio, sin violencia: Una historia personal del NO*. Santiago: Ariel, 2013.

"TVN a 40 años del golpe: el documental que complica al Directorio del 'canal de todos.'" *El Dínamo* (August 22, 2013). http://www.eldinamo.cl/cultpop/2013/08/22/tvn-a-40-anos-del-golpe-el-documental-que-complica-al-directorio-del-canal-de-todos/.

Uribe, Armando and Miguel Vicuña. *El accidente Pinochet*. Santiago: Editorial Sudamericana, 1999.

Valdés, Hernán. *Tejas Verdes: Diario de un campo de concentración en Chile*. Santiago: LOM Ediciones, 2003.

Vinyes, Ricard. "Sobre Londres 38." *El País* (October 10, 2007).

Virno, Paolo. *Déjà Vu and the End of History*. Trans. David Broder. London: Verso, 2015.

Index

Note: locators followed by *f* refer to figures.

activism, xi
in Chile, xxiv
commissions and tribunals,
27, 82, 132, 149
groups, xx, 8, 57, 167n18
movements, 71, 81
Universal Declaration of
Human Rights, 87–8
violations of, xxv, 25–6, 36,
45, 47, 72, 82, 85, 103,
105, 108–10, 113, 115,
128, 135–6, 139, 141–4,
146, 149–50, 157n5,
166n9, 170n7
see also Museo de la Memoria
y los Derechos Humanos
[Museum of Memory and
Human Rights]

identity, 6–7, 9, 15, 32, 34–7,
58, 65–6, 68, 81, 138, 143
as absence, 80
control of, 112
gender as, xiv, 34
mistaken, 79
mortification of, 73
national, 88
non-identity, 77, 113
seizure of, 106–8
social, 154n2
inscription, 82, 116, 121
of memory, 11, 82
of the present, xi
of the proper name, 47
institutionalization, xvi–xvii,
xix, 88, 143
intellectuals, xi–xvii, 153n1
International Day of the
Disappeared, 103–6, 110f,
113

Kristeva, Julia, xv, 15

Lagos, Ricardo, 105, 127, 142

language, 24, 30, 44, 50, 71, 84
advertising and, 94, 96
of art collections, 85
audiovisual, 91
of cultural criticism, xxv
everyday, 42
figurative, 3
of governmental interests, 13
memory and, 9, 149
of photographic images, 21
remorseful, 29
theoretical, xvi
torture and, 52, 134; see also
speech
of the Transition, xxiv–xxv, 4
Larraín, Hernán, 144, 170n6
Larraín, Pablo, 92–8, 102,
161n2, 161–2n4, 162n6,
162n13, 163n17
No, 92–8, 102, 161n4,
162n6, 162–3n13
see also García Bernal, Gael
Latin America, x–xiv, xvi, xviii
US intervention in, 122
utopias of, 140
Lavín, Joaquín, 99–100, 102
limit experience, 64, 134
torture as, 36, 73, 133
Londres 38, 83–87
Londres 38 Memory Space,
103
see also Colectivo Londres
38
loss, xxv, 4–5, 8–10, 77–8,
117, 119
of freedom, 170n7
imaginary of, 113
of life, 122
of one's being, 55
of revolutionary horizon, xx
of speech, 36

Mapuche
conflict, 106, 108–9, 143